VOYAGE TO GALAPAGOS

VOYAGE TO
GALAPAGOS

by

WILLIAM
ALBERT ROBINSON

Author of *Deep Water and Shoal*

With drawings by
DANIEL T. WEST

JONATHAN CAPE
THIRTY BEDFORD SQUARE
LONDON

FIRST PUBLISHED 1936

JONATHAN CAPE LTD. 30 BEDFORD SQUARE, LONDON
AND 91 WELLINGTON STREET WEST, TORONTO

PRINTED IN GREAT BRITAIN IN THE CITY OF OXFORD
AT THE ALDEN PRESS
PAPER MADE BY JOHN DICKINSON & CO., LTD.
BOUND BY A. W. BAIN & CO., LTD.

TO
THE UNITED STATES NAVY
AND TO
TWELVE FISHERMEN OF THE
SANTA CRUZ

CONTENTS

7

ILLUSTRATIONS

VOYAGE TO GALAPAGOS

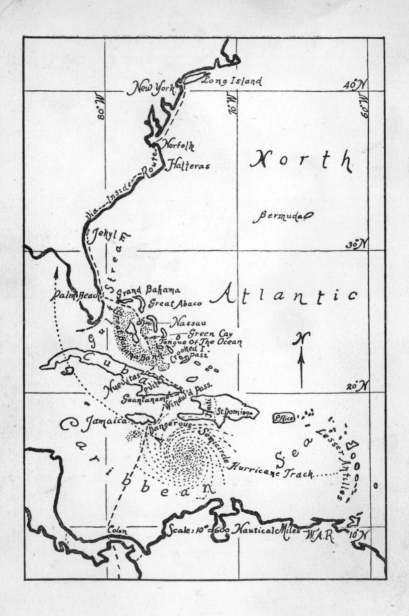

CHAPTER I

THE END OF AN INTERLUDE

IT just missed being an arctic expedition, to the white icy wastes of the North-West Passage. My head was full of the thousand and one details that go with the organization of such a venture. The backbone of the depression was broken. The financial backing seemed assured.

Then came ominous warnings. The bank moratorium and a wave of failures swept the country. The backing which had been promised was strangely delayed, at last definitely withdrawn. On that day—one of those days when a word or two changes the entire plan of your life—the new voyage was born. I had been a landlubber a year and a half, and anyone with the flavour of salt in his blood and the wanderlust, and a sailor at heart, knows that a year and a half is altogether too long to be ashore, even though one is not idle. Lord knows I had not been idle, for I had written, lectured, and married the only girl in the world who could have shared this crazy life of mine and loved it.

And so that day the decision was made — in less time than it takes to tell. It would be the Galapagos. I could write the book which I had already started when in those islands before. We would make a short moving picture that had been proposed. Our hearts throbbed with excitement. The hurricane season would soon be upon us and there was no time to waste.

In a little inlet on the outskirts of sleepy Port Washington, snug and secure, the *Svaap* rose and fell with the slow breathing of the tide, dreaming of her past exploits. We went out there, Florence and I, on the morning after the day of decision, and told the news to *Svaap*: that she was going again where the trade winds blew, to the isles of the far South Seas. And we scrubbed her and painted her and filled her full of food and gear until everything was ready.

The opinion of our families was fixed and undeviating. At first, when they heard that our plans for the Arctic were indefinitely postponed, there was a sigh of relief all round. But then, when we announced our imminent departure for the Galapagos, in a thirty-two-foot ketch, there were a hundred new objections.

'It's unheard-of,' they cried in despair. 'You simply *can't* take a girl like that on such a trip!'

When I reminded them that I had taken *Svaap* completely around the world in safety in all kinds of weather, they snorted. That was different. I was used to hardships, while she had always had all the comforts and luxuries conceivable. In vain I explained that because she *had* had all these things was the very reason that she knew how unnecessary they are to fundamental happiness. She was healthy and strong. She was slender, possibly frail in appearance, but that exterior is often a disguise for people whose inner fire and nervous energy carry them on to far greater feats of endurance than those with black-smith or Amazonian bodies. As a girl she had lived by the wide, white dunes of Ipswich, and there on the Massachusetts coast she had learned to sail. She knew what it meant to go to sea in a small ketch. Those who have made ocean passages in small craft will know what this means. Knowing, she *wanted* to go and had as much to do with our decision to go as I had. But nothing would convince our families that I was not carrying out a great folly. I would bring her back a wreck if I brought her back at all. We closed our ears and took *Svaap* through Hell Gate to Staten Island, where we lay along-side Bob Bartlett's *Morrissey* which was outfitting for a Greenland voyage.

It was Sunday, June 11th, 1933. Those last minute repairs, without which no expedition could possibly depart, had been completed the night before. The silent deserted shipyard suddenly became a hive of activity. News-reel lorries rolled out on the dock. Reporters came in twos and threes, some with studied casualness, some hardboiled and noisy, others quiet and efficient.

The heat poured down like rain falling from a tropical squall. It reflected from the iron surface of the pier in shimmering waves. Coats were off, sleeves rolled up, and sweat poured from the impatient news-reel men. Tempers had an edge.

Our sails were up and we were free — free at last — nosing through the oil-covered waters of the slip. A fresh cool breeze whipped out of the Kill Van Kull. We heeled to the strength of it and raced out with the tide toward the Narrows.

I looked back at the little crowd there on the pier — at the tri-legged monsters that turned their baleful glassy stare upon us that the world might see and hear the departure of *Svaap* for the Galapagos. A feeling of revulsion, then indescribable relief swept over me. Thank God *that's* over with. No publicity? they had cried a few days before. Why, you've *got* to have it — it's indispensable — you can't do anything without it. . . . My mind flew back to that other voyage, when we sailed unknown, without huzzas. We had crept in and out of ports silently, following the ways of the sea for three and a half years, circling the world and completing the voyage before a single news-reel was shot. *That* was the way! Do your job without hullabaloo, complete it successfully, and then — if you want — tell the world about it. But this premature fuss and bother was all wrong. My sailor's intuition whispered to me that it was a bad beginning.

And it was a bad beginning, for as we tacked through the Narrows into Gravesend Bay, Dan began to complain of a swollen foot. By the time we were well into Ambrose Channel, with Sandy Hook abeam, it was obviously in need of lancing and we anchored behind Coney Island to get a doctor. A false start . . . the worst possible omen for a voyage!

We sailed the following day. We were three aboard. Florence, as I have said, had sailed a good deal, although she had never really been at sea in quite so small a craft. She was, and always has been, as immune to seasickness as I am. My cousin, Dan West, our twenty-year-old artist-cook, was new to the sea.

A wicked squall swept out of the south before we had even reached Barnegat, kicking up a cross sea and killing the good west wind. We tumbled and pitched in a calm. Six feet of artist concentrated upon a very unartistic performance at the rail. A bank of lowering black clouds closed down from the north and soon there was wind, a hard norther. For two days we ran before it with a wicked sea pounding under our counter, and anchored in Norfolk to give my weary crew a rest.

It had been a strenuous but successful initiation for all. After a bad hour or so Dan was with us again and watches were fairly divided between the three. Even in the beginning, in this bad weather, my much-worried-about Florence proved herself capable of handling *Svaap* like a veteran, and during the entire voyage that followed stood her watches regularly without fail. The picture in my mind remains to-day as clear as it was those days on the Atlantic, and later on the hurricane-threatening Caribbean or the rolling blue Pacific. It is the picture of a slender girl standing at the wheel, bracing herself against the heave of the little ketch, soft golden hair whipping free in the breeze, blue eyes gazing steadily ahead to a distant horizon, and now and then at the compass or aloft at the sails. In her lonely night watch she would sing at the wheel to give herself courage as she steered on and on into a black void, keeping the rhythm of the cresting seas as they rushed under the counter. From my bunk I could see her there — the light of the binnacle casting a faint glow upon the oval of her face, vaguely suggesting her delicate features. A rush of warm confidence and pride in this girl of mine would sweep over me and I would fall asleep listening to the rush of water on the other side of the planking by my head, and to the soft notes of her song that drifted down the companionway.

CHAPTER II

'JULY—STAND BY'

July — stand by
August — if you must
September — remember
October — all over[1]

Down the east coast of the United States, threading its devious way through tidal estuaries, sounds, rivers, and man-made canals, stretches the inland waterway system, little known by Americans in general but free to all. Here small craft may sail all the way from New York to Key West in protected waters. Meandering intimately the length of seven states, it offers a unique and inexpensive vacation to anyone with a boat of not more than six or

[1] The Mariners' warning to sailors in the Caribbean Sea.

seven feet draught. Why more people do not avail themselves of the opportunity I do not understand.

We entered the waterway at Norfolk and headed south,
avoiding Hatteras. The days that followed were peaceful
and pleasant as we picked our way through Virginia,
North and South Carolina, and Georgia. Dismal Swamp
. . . Albemarle Sound . . . Pamlico Sound . . . Bogue Sound
. . . Cape Fear River . . . one after the other they slipped
behind, the ghosts of Captain Kidd, Blackbeard the Pirate,
and all the others little disturbed by our passing. Charles-
ton. Then on through Coosaw River, Brickyard Creek
(imagine an ocean-crossing ketch in Brickyard Creek) . . .
and so on to Jekyl Island where we went outside and
coasted along to Palm Beach where we were to leave the
American coast for good.

We were very late. The norther that had blown us into
Norfolk was the last fair wind we had until nearing Panama. All through the canals we had bucked head winds
and it was not until the evening of July 10th, already the
beginning of the hurricane season, that we finally took our
departure from Palm Beach for Nassau.

That night we had a gentle southerly breeze and raced
across the Gulf Stream with the engine at full speed to aid
the sails. We sighted Grand Bahama before the wind
came in hard ahead and drove the squalls down upon us.

Squalls — squalls — squalls! For two days and nights
we had nothing else. Squalls that drove all our canvas
down and threw up enormous quantities of water. Squalls
with the most continuous, blinding lightning I have ever

seen. Squalls that all came from the south and made every mile a struggle.

Then, on the dawn of the third day, with the harbour of Nassau in sight, the weather changed. While Dan slept, exhausted from his hard four-hour watch, I perched on the cross-trees and conned her in between the reefs with Florence at the wheel, sailing her under all canvas with a gentle perfume-laden breeze from the land. It was the hour I love perhaps most of all on the water. A new day dawning. A cool morning breeze off the land bearing the scent of its flowers, and the peaceful sounds of a town awakening.

The water was transparent. The vivid deep blues had become emerald, and beneath was the coral. When I looked down and saw our anchor chain snaking its way along the colourful bottom — five fathoms below — I felt at last that we had reached our old haunts. It could almost have been the Pacific, that sea I love the best of all.

We were now definitely in the hurricane belt. I have seen two of these great storms and have an almighty respect for them. I had no intention of getting caught at sea in one. Our route to Panama lay through the Bahamas, Cuba, and Jamaica. The breeding place of the hurricanes lies well to the south of this route, and with the present system of wirelessing storm information there would be ample time to seek shelter between the first warning and the time the hurricane reached our latitude. Thus we were to be very dependent upon weather reports until reaching Panama. But we had no wireless. Every inch of space was packed with the essentials of food and equipment. I felt confident, however, that by stopping frequently, wherever we could get wireless reports, we would be in no danger. Thus our decision to stop in Nassau, Cuba, and Jamaica, even though we were in a great hurry to get to Panama and away from the dangerous area.

The Palm Beach report was favourable, but Nassau reported a disturbance of great intensity to the south of Haiti. For four days we watched this storm sweep slowly north, wondering if it would pass our way. When it was safely in the Gulf of Mexico we hurried out of Nassau. Against my better judgment — which told me to swing outside and make for the Windward Passage via Crooked Island, through open waters — I listened to the advice of a Nassau captain and took a short cut through the Tongue of the Ocean, Blossom Channel, and over the Great Bahama Bank. We would anchor each night and sail by day. The reefs would be easily seen, for the water was clear. The weather would be fine at this season, he assured us, so long as no major disturbance was in the vicinity. We could not know that down to the south — in a little-frequented region — the grim forces of a new storm were already gathering.

So south through the reefs we sailed. The first day the trade wind held good, and we anchored on a shoal at the edge of the Tongue of the Ocean, with its 800 fathom depth. But the night became black, and the barometer was not right. A vicious wind with increasing gusts tore at us. The lacy chain of cays to the east were scant protection and those to leeward were a growing danger. We rode to fifty fathoms of chain and all night jerked and tore at it in the rising sea. At dawn Florence took her position at the wheel and Dan and I went to the pitching bow to struggle with the chain—that back-breaking chain that was slack one moment, jerking bar-taut the next. Careful! Careful! That chain can tear flesh and break bones. . . .

The anchor came aboard. *Svaap* fell off and drove south again. We must time our arrival at dangerous Blossom Channel just right. It must be early morning. So at Green Cay that afternoon we anchored for a brief respite until dark came again. Then during the night we sailed across the very tip of the Tongue of the Ocean, still with the same threatening weather.

Morning found us tacking through Blossom Channel, rail awash, down to lowers. Another night, this time hove to under a scrap of sail, only fifteen miles from the reef-infested southern exit from the Great Bahama Bank. It was a wild night, and a wild dirty grey morning when we again got under way. I climbed to the upper cross-trees. Dan stood by the sheets. Florence held the wheel, her lips tight, tense in every nerve.

It was the last ten miles we dreaded — ten miles of lurking winding reefs and of isolated coral heads hidden beneath a few feet of water, ready to tear the bottom out of your ship. I am an experienced coral pilot, having done this sort of thing all through the South Pacific, but this was one of the worst stretches I've ever done. Heavy wind. Rough sea, but not enough swell to break on shoals a fathom deep. Dirty grey light instead of good sunlight to reveal the colour difference between the deep water and the dangerous shallows.

We were heeled so far that I stood with one foot on the narrow cross-trees, and the other braced against the mast itself. With each lurch, as we hit a wave, I tensed my whole body and clung with all my strength as the mast whipped forward. I looked down at my little ship, at my crew who had never seen this sort of thing before, yet never showed a moment of fear.

My eyes strained, trying to pierce the surface of the sea. A vague suggestion of darker colour — just a faint smudge — dead ahead.

'Ready about. Hard starboard!' We shot around. Halyards whipped at me. I slid around to the other side of the mast and braced myself for the lunge when she filled again. The smudge slid past a length to port. We drove on. Another smudge ahead, a bigger one this time.

'Ready about! No! No! Steady on your course.' For it was moving . . . a reflection of that black racing cloud overhead, not a ragged edged reef. Another smudge, coral this time again. . . .

'Hard aport!' Score two in our favour. On we tore, white water under our bow, rail always awash. This was living! This *was* a game. Blow wind, blow! Ahead was a long line of white — the open sea pounding on the last line of reefs — the last of the Great Bahama Bank. Beyond was safety and freedom, and Cuba across the Strait. No straining of eyes for these reefs . . . their white spouting fountains shot thirty feet high, their thunder came to us already.

'A little to port — hold it — Steady now, steer for that opening!'

We pitched and jerked no longer. We sailed up and over a long deep-water sea. I relaxed my vice-like hold on mast and rigging and slid down to deck. Twenty-four hours later we anchored off Nuevitas, Cuba, just long enough to receive a weather report which checked with my suspicions. A tropical disturbance was reported moving north in our direction. It was the cause of our upset weather. It might strike Cuba.

There was much better hurricane protection a day's sail up the coast at Port Vita, and plenty of time to get there with the storm still two or three days away. We plunged along the Cuban coast against a heavy sea, hove to half the next night when it blew too hard to carry any driving sail, and nearly pounded the masts out driving her the following day to make port before dark. A heavy haze hung low. The mountains near Gibara were close abeam before we saw them looming faint and indistinct. Vita was just beyond, a tiny inconspicuous inlet, difficult to find. Again I went aloft.

A clump of palms leaned over the entrance, a thatch hut across the way. The narrow winding stream opened after about a mile into a roomy basin with a huge storehouse and an imposing pier, with houses beyond. We anchored and at last felt secure.

We had expected to go direct from Nassau to the American Naval Base at Guantanamo, and so had no papers for Vita. Due to the approaching storm we made an emergency entrance seeking refuge. This completely disorganized the Port Vita officials. They grew hysterical but not inarticulate. It was forbidden to enter a Cuban port without a clearance for that port! We *must* have it — it could not be otherwise!

I pointed out that we had entered the port under stress of weather — an international privilege — and that we intended to remain until the hurricane had passed. We would not go ashore if they did not wish us to.

The officials departed with ominous shakings of the head, only slightly more friendly after consuming liberally of our liquid hospitality, taking with them various of our ship's papers. They would telephone Gibara for instructions. Apparently Gibara was the head office for the district. Later they returned. We could go ashore, but were not allowed to leave until instructions came from Havana via Gibara. We were delighted. In two or three days the hurricane would be past. By then we would have arranged things by wire through the legation at Havana or the authorities at Guantanamo. We did not know that the revolution was about to overwhelm Machado and that the country-wide unrest was the cause of the strange tenseness of everyone in Vita. We did not know that we were suspected of some political intrigue and that we would not be permitted the use of the wires.

CHAPTER III

SANTA LUCIA—'YOU SHALL SEE MY BEAUTIFUL HOUSE'

VITA was the shipping port of the powerful Santa Lucia sugar company. It contained only the storehouses, the pier, a few houses of employees and government officials, and the barracks. A few miles inland, over a narrow gauge track, lay the town of Santa Lucia with its 3000 inhabitants, all connected with the sugar company. The Santa Lucia domain stretched for miles, dominating this section of the country. Master of it all, we were told, was a Señor 'Felucca' Sanchez.

On the morning of the third day, a little car arrived

with a considerable *éclat* at the Vita end of the narrow gauge. Its shrill whistle announced that Señor Sanchez had arrived to call. Accompanied by several henchmen, he came aboard, attired in riding clothes, boots, and picturesque sombrero. A large revolver was strapped to his waist. He was handsome, American-educated, a bit condescending, very suave and full of Latin *politesse*. Here was the man, we thought, who could straighten out our port difficulties.

They drank our liquor, accepted our cigarettes, showed keen interest in our voyage, examined everything. We outdid ourselves in hospitality. Señor Sanchez became talkative. He described his beautiful home to us. Our iceless drinks reminded him of his huge American electric refrigerator and of the tall icy drinks that were served at his house. He described his luxurious American plumbing and the cool showers which he could have when hot and sticky from the heat.

Our mouths were watering, and we could already feel the cool shower caressing our sweating bodies. Our last cold drink had been in Nassau — bath also. We admitted this to Señor Sanchez. Since our arrival in Vita a deadening calm had held night and day — the approaching hurricane had caused it — and a ceaseless sickening heat had persisted, along with the gnats and mosquitoes. If only he would invite us to . . .

'You must return with me to Santa Lucia,' he urged just then. 'You shall see my beautiful house!'

Clackety-clack. Clackety-clack. We rushed through

the sweltering jungle-like growth of the vast plantations. Señor Sanchez waved his arm.

'It is all ours', he said.

Our eyes looked at miles of rolling fertility but instead we saw a big cool flower-banked house with showers and tall icy drinks, and Cuban hospitality at its best.

Santa Lucia! We stepped from the noisy little railcar into dust which rose in a stifling cloud about us. Sanchez led the way uphill past the poor frame-houses of the workers. The heat was dreadful there but we were sustained by that cool shower and those tall icy drinks.

We reached the top. A pretty little park. A fresh cool breeze. There, commanding the scene, looking out over the park and across the valley to the rolling hills and the sea beyond, stood Señor Sanchez's house, freshly painted and bowered in flowers as he had said.

'Is it not beautiful?' He gazed at it with pride.

It was lovely, it was sublime, it was heaven itself, we said as we started eagerly forward. Señor Sanchez walked a little to one side.

'Come! From here the view is best of all, I think.'

Again we looked — and agreed that it was magnificent.

'And now', he apologized, 'if you will excuse, I must leave you. You would like a bath? Ah! I thought so. — Pedro! Come here. — My man will take you to a bath. There is a shower in the unused men's barracks down the hill. Adios, Señora. Adios, Señor.'

And he left, no doubt to go to his cool shower, and his tall icy drink.

27

The peon started off downhill, turned and saw us standing in the same spot. Perhaps we had not understood.

'Señor. Down there we go'. He pointed down into the sweltering breathless houses below. We stumbled after him through the dust, and came to a deserted dilapidated building. There was a large rusty padlock on the door. The windows were boarded.

Pedro made a Latin shrug. He had no key. He thought a while.

'Ah, Señor, come'.

Again we followed, and once more perspired our way up the weary dusty hill to Señor Sanchez's house with the modern plumbing and cool showers. But we did not stop. We walked on past, to the other side of the hill where stood a long ramshackle building containing stores, post office, and company offices. We climbed stairs. There at last was a rusty shower, complete with cobwebs, spiders of enormous girth, and broken glass from the window. We bathed in a rusty warm trickle and climbed into our sticky clothes.

We went out and on to the Sanchez house to inquire about returning to Port Vita. We walked up the steps and from behind the door sprang a soldier with menacing bayonet, barring the way. At the office by the narrow gauge railway we found an English-speaking clerk.

'Si, Si, Señor Sanchez has issued instructions that the train is at your disposal. One dollar it costs, for each. What? Oh, you wish to eat. Si, si, Señor. In the town is a public restaurant. There you will find meat and frijoles. At five the train will be back. Adios, Señor!'

We ate, poorly. We walked. Becoming aware that a soldier followed us everywhere, we leaned against a fence to rest, tired. The soldier sprang forward.

'Se prohibe!' he gesticulated, and at length we realized that it was our leaning against the fence that he objected to. We stopped leaning and took to walking again. We had until five to wait. We again became weary and sat down on the kerb in the shade of a tree. The guard again sprang forward, rifle in hand, ugly, menacing.

'Se prohibe!'

The camel's back broke. Regardless of consequences I leaped to my feet loud with profanity and told the man with suitable adjectives where to go. I all but struck him. He understood not a word, except perhaps the epithets — but he knew what I meant. His arrogant, overbearing attitude suddenly wilted and to our utter amazement he crept away to watch us from the corner.

It was so completely incongruous and unexpected that we laughed until the tears came. Typical of his species — suspicious, taking no pains to conceal his Latin-American hatred of Americans, domineering when he had the upper hand, he was coward at heart. It had been an ugly situation. A few people collected. The man looked so ridiculous that Dan got out his sketch pad and started to draw him in caricature. Men looked over Dan's shoulder and laughed. Florence started sign talk with a dilapidated-looking individual. The soldier became ludicrously self-conscious and embarrassed, tried a sickly grin and sheepishly withdrew from sight behind a building and ceased to follow us.

We returned to Port Vita at five. We never saw the inside of Señor Sanchez's house.

CHAPTER IV

HASTA LA VISTA

THE hurricane had passed to the east heading toward Nassau. There was a wonderful fair wind which would take us down to Cape Maysi and the Windward Passage a-flying. Soon it would fail, and the trade wind would return. Then it would be a long weary job against a head wind. Every hour we wasted at Vita was tragedy.

The port officials were in an insolent mood. For four days we had talked — talked — talked, in the stifling tin-roofed office of the *aduana*, trying to get our papers back and permission to leave. A guard stood on the pier by day and by night. I cajoled. I tried all forms of

persuasion and flattery. I quoted international marine law.
I became furious and threatened. All had the same effect:
nothing.

'Mañana', the aduana would say. 'Mañana I shall
receive instructions from Gibara.'

'But you have been talking to Gibara on the phone for
four days now', I would cry, on the verge of mental
disintegration.

'Si, Señor. But Gibara must receive instructions from
Havana.'

I dragged Florence into it and she applied feminine
wiles. She begged and pleaded and smiled and flattered.
She even wept.

We wrote telegrams to the Commandant of the American Naval Base at Guantanamo and to the legation at
Havana. They politely took our money and never sent
the messages. The long distance phone, they said, was
out of order. We were, to all intents and purposes,
prisoners, *incommunicado*.

I had noticed that when the day guard went off for
supper the relief was usually a little late. There was an
unguarded period of perhaps five minutes. We decided
to run for it, and leave our papers with them. They had
no boat with which to follow. Several years before, in
Arabia, I had run *Svaap* out from under the noses of
Bedouin captors. Probably we could do it again.

During the afternoon we sneaked our anchor chain in
until it was straight up and down. I overhauled the
engine. We made a little fort out of spare sails and gear,

to protect the helmsman, and flew the American flag conspicuously, hoping that they would not dare to fire upon it, and thinking that even if they did they probably couldn't hit anything anyway.

When the guard went off to supper I sent Florence below. We quietly got in the rest of the chain and touched the starter. The engine roared as I threw the throttle as far ahead as it would go. The *Svaap* spun on her heel and gathered way.

Florence's excited blonde head kept popping out of the cabin like a jack-in-the-box in spite of orders. Dan lay on deck behind the cabin house and I crouched behind the shelter, steering for the turn into the narrow stream. Surely they had heard the motor by now. Any moment they would appear and order us to stop. But would they shoot?

We passed the first channel buoy. The second. Just as we shot into the narrows several soldiers raced down on the pier brandishing their rifles. Then we were out of sight around the bend.

It was dark when we emerged from the inlet and headed down the coast. We were free. Far behind twinkled the lights of Gibara. How I had learned to hate its very name. A little later I happened to glance astern, and there, heading straight for us, I saw the lights of a large vessel. She had obviously come from Gibara. Good Lord! It was the Cuban gunboat we had heard of and forgotten. They had telephoned the news of our escape from Port Vita and sent the gunboat after us. Now we *were* in for it.

The one-sided race began. We again pushed the engine to the limit. We put out all lights and hugged the coast as close as we dared, hoping that they would miss us in the dark. An hour went by — a tense hopeless hour — for she crept slowly up on us. We changed our course and a little later she followed. Well. Only a few more moments now!

Not one of us said a word. I was racking my brain for a good dignified way to surrender a thirty-two-foot ketch to a gunboat. She came up close alongside, her engines clanking . . . and passed on out of sight ahead — an old ocean tramp going about her own business. She had never seen us. Oh! what a guilty conscience can do.

Again we took up the threads of our voyage. We must get to Guantanamo with no delay for the wireless reports. Perhaps a new storm was brewing. The following night we reached the turning point of the voyage to Panama — Cape Maysi and the Windward Passage. I remembered sailing through the Passage on the first voyage of *Svaap*. We had gone through backwards riding out a gale to a sea-anchor. This strait is often a wicked place for small boats. But this time our luck was in, and the strait was kind.

The trade wind blew fresh all night and carried us through the uneasy, current-swept waters of the Passage, so that morning found us coasting along the leeward side of Cuba, beneath its tall green mountains.

Guantanamo was exceedingly hospitable, but we hastened on with a good weather report. The trade wind blew hard from the south-east and carried us in two days to

Jamaica, that old pirate rendezvous. How well I knew the channel into Kingston! Five years before, to the very day, almost the very hour, I had entered the historic old port and anchored beneath its lofty Blue Mountains. At Port Royal we anchored again in the same old place.

CHAPTER V

'AUGUST—IF YOU MUST'

SVAAP pitched and tossed to a rising wind in the poor protection of Kingston Harbour. My instinct told me another hurricane was brewing although the weather report held no warnings as yet. I believe in my intuitions, and we acted without delay on this one. Two hundred miles on the way to Panama and we would be out of the track of the hurricanes. Two hundred miles that became the measure between safety and something else. We sailed abruptly, without waiting even for fresh provisions. Two or three days after we left Jamaica, a hurricane swept in from the Caribbean and went straight through Kingston. We got out just in time.

When we nosed out from behind Port Royal we met a long ominous swell. The barometer was jumpy and uncertain. Later it began to fall slowly. In the tropics there is a regular daily tidal movement (the diurnal oscillation) of the barometer, by which seamen know that all is well. Twice each day, at 10 a.m. and 10 p.m., there is a period of high pressure. At 4 a.m. and 4 p.m. it is low. If the regularity of this oscillation is broken something unusual is stirring. From July to October in the West Indies it is apt to be a cyclonic disturbance — otherwise known as *hurricane*. So the action of our barometer, added to the swell that was running, made me all the more certain that somewhere to the east one of the great storms was coming — probably from the region below Martinique and Barbados, the malevolent womb where the majority of these West Indian catastrophes are conceived.

The hurricane was probably at least three days away. The pilot chart showed that of all the storm tracks for August plotted since 1887, not one traversed the region south of latitude 15. These storms are fortunately quite dependable, following well defined tracks. In other words, if we sailed southwards on our course to Panama for forty-eight hours we would emerge from the region subject to hurricanes in general and this one in particular. If the coming storm — I was sure it was one — was still several hundred miles to the east, that left us just about the necessary time to run off our two hundred miles to safety before the weather got too bad to carry sail. It would be close though.

We staggered along under every rag she could carry, making heavy weather of it. A great mass of cloud rose above the horizon to the east, small patches tearing away and bringing down squalls of rain and increasing wind . . . the advance winds of the hurricane itself. The hurricane is a circular area of winds of terrific velocity, revolving spirally in a counter-clockwise direction[1] around a central area of low barometric pressure, the whole system covering a diameter of possibly three hundred miles for the gale winds, while the actual diameter of the violent destructive hurricane winds is often less than a hundred miles. The whole system advances leisurely at a speed of eight or ten miles an hour for the first while, working west and north, increasing its rate of advance to twenty or thirty miles an hour as it reaches more northerly latitudes. On it marches, day after day, until it has covered a thousand or two thousand miles and wearies of it all, dispersing somewhere on the American coast or in the North Atlantic. On the right-hand side of the centre of advance (called the dangerous semicircle) the winds are more dangerous than on the left-hand side. In the very centre there is the vortex — an area ten to twenty miles wide of calm and blue sky, but an unhappy calm for the seaman, for it is there that the

[1] This and all following information pertains to the northern hemisphere. The rules for hurricanes in the southern hemisphere are always exactly the reverse.

seas are worst, thrown in with overwhelming violence from all directions, presenting the greatest menace of all. After a short interval the wind will burst with hurricane force from a point directly opposite to that from which it was blowing before. There is a fascination though, in this little spot of calm air, surrounded by its whirling fury of the most terrible winds known to the world — the 'eye of the storm'. Some mariners have returned, full of awe . . . others have not returned.

I read feverishly in my manual, comparing our weather symptoms with those described for hurricanes. They checked all too well. I studied again and again the directions for avoiding the centre — directions I all but knew by heart from other trying experiences. Now they became disconnected and hard to co-ordinate. If there is anything in print more depressing to read in a crisis than the literature pertaining to hurricanes I hope I never run across it. In between the doleful warnings and accounts of distressed ten-thousand-ton vessels were useful bits of information.

. . . A long swell from the direction of the storm usually sets in before any other indication becomes marked.

When the sky first becomes overcast with the characteristic veil of cirrus, the storm centre will most probably lie in the direction of the greatest density of the cloud.

When the hurricane cloud appears over the horizon it will be densest at the storm centre.

By this time the barometer will usually be showing

unmistakable evidence of a fall, and one may confidently look for a storm and begin observations to determine the location of its centre and the direction in which it is moving.

Surrounding the actual storm area is a territory of large extent throughout which the barometer reads a tenth of an inch or more below the average, the pressure diminishing toward the central area, but with no such rapidity as is noted within that area itself. Throughout the outer ring unsettled weather prevails. The sky is ordinarily covered with a light haze, which increases in density as the centre of the storm approaches. Showers are frequent. Throughout the northern semicircle of this area the wind rises to force 6 or 8 — the 'reinforced trades' — and is accompanied by squalls. Throughout the other semicircle unsettled winds, generally from a southeasterly direction, prevail.

It is very important to determine as early as possible the location and direction of travel of the centre.

The relation between the position of the ship and the position and prospective track of the centre will indicate the proper course to pursue:

(*a*) to enable the vessel to keep out of or escape from the dangerous semicircle and to avoid the centre of the storm;

(*b*) to enable the vessel to ride it out in safety if unable to escape from it.

Should the ship be to the westward of the storm centre it may be assumed that the latter will draw nearer more or less directly. [We were, and it did.] It then becomes of the utmost importance to determine its path and so learn whether the vessel is in the right or left semicircle.

The winds in that semicircle which is more remote from the equator (the right-hand side in the
northern hemisphere) are liable to be more severe
than those of the opposite semicircle. A vessel hove-
to in the semicircle adjacent to the equator has also the
advantage of immunity from becoming involved in
the actual centre itself, for there is a distinct tendency
for the storm to move away from the equator and to
recurve. Thus the right-hand semicircle has been
called the *dangerous*, while the left-hand side is called
the *navigable*.

A vessel hove-to in advance of a tropical storm
will experience a long heavy swell, a falling barometer with torrents of rain and winds of increasing
force. The shifts of wind will depend upon the
position of the vessel with respect to the track
followed by the storm centre. Immediately upon the
track, the wind will hold steady in direction until the
passage of the central calm, the 'eye of the storm',
after which the gale will renew itself, but from a
direction opposite to that which it previously had.
To the right of the track, or in the right-hand semicircle of the storm, the wind, as the centre advances
and passes the vessel, will constantly shift to the
right, the rate at which the successive shifts follow
each other increasing with the proximity to the
centre; in this semicircle, then, in order that the
wind shall draw aft with each shift, and the vessel
not be taken aback, a sailing vessel must be hove-to
on the starboard tack; similarly, in the left-hand semicircle, the wind will constantly shift to the left, and
here a sailing vessel must be hove-to on the port tack
so as not to be taken aback. These rules hold for both
hemispheres and for cyclonic storms in all latitudes.

Since the wind circulates counterclockwise in the northern hemisphere, the rule is to face the wind and the storm centre will be on the right hand. If the wind travelled in exact circles, the centre would be eight points to the right when looking directly in the wind's eye. However, the wind follows more or less a spiral path inward, which brings the centre from eight to twelve points to the right of the direction of the wind. The number of points to the right may vary during the same storm, and as the wind usually shifts in squalls, its direction should be taken just after a squall.

Ten points to the right when facing the wind is a good average allowance to make if in front of the storm.

Two bearings of the centre with an interval between of from two to three hours will, in general, be sufficient to determine the course of the storm. Should the wind not shift, but continue to blow steadily with increasing force, and with a falling barometer, it may be assumed that the vessel is on or near the storm track.

The distance away from the storm centre can only be estimated very imperfectly. One can only guess at the distance of the centre by the height of the barometer and its rate of fall.

There were a hundred complications and possibilities for error in judgment, detailed instructions on what to do if actually overtaken. It all boiled down to the fact that according to my guess, applying the rules to our local conditions, we were directly in front of the storm centre, still two or three days away; that the obvious manœuvre was to run to the south to avoid the dangerous semicircle and the centre and to be in the *navigable* semicircle in case my confidence was unwarranted and we were unable actually to outrun the area of violent winds entirely. I was pretty sure though, that with the good start we had, we could get south fast enough to escape with only a bad dusting, skirting the advancing edge of the storm region, ultimately easing out to the south while the real hurricane swept across where we had been in the beginning. It only meant being able to carry sail for another thirty-six hours, heading a little west of south, fortunately directly on our course to Panama. It was vital that there should be no mistake anywhere in our calculation — for otherwise we would be in trouble with the reefs and cays of Pedro Bank, or the other similar dangers farther to the south-west.

So we drove the *Svaap* as she has rarely been driven, with a rising gale and an enormous sea abeam. The sky was a gloomy leaden vault. At sunset there was that beautiful golden haze in the sky that is the forerunner of hurricanes. I did not leave the wheel that night, for a less experienced helmsman might not have met the largest of those destructive seas just right. One mistake would have been fatal. It was by no means easier on the others, probably much worse in fact, for I at least had a considerable occupation while they had to be shut up in a gyrating little cabin with the noises of doomsday about their ears as the seas crashed on the planking over and around them, and the boat groaned and strained. As the night wore on the deadweight of uncertainty and anxiety piled up in proportion as the seas piled up higher and higher, and the voice of the wind in the stays beside me rose until it became a super-dentist's drill boring away at my nerves, already worn from the strain of four weeks in the hell-cauldron of the West Indies during one of the worst hurricane seasons in many years. We should have been through to Panama long before it all began, but we had been for ever haunted by an evil genius who held us back and made every mile a fight. Three hurricanes already — each one closer. And this last one — how close would *it* come? What if my calculations were wrong and we were driving headlong with the utmost force we could use and not tear apart the fabric of the ship — *into* the dangerous semicircle instead of out of it as I believed we were. Why had I been obsessed by this urge to drive on and on. *July* — *stand by; August* — *if you must* . . . the words of the ditty kept ringing in my head. *August* — *if you must* . . . but why must we . . . we could have nosed in somewhere, some land-locked little inlet, and waited until the season was over. But no — we must push on, on, beat the season and get to the Galapagos that much sooner. Before, on the first voyage, I had taken chances too, occasionally but not often, and had not worried overmuch. But suddenly now the added responsibility of Florence and Dan brought on a wave of remorse. I learned that night a new lesson — that the saving of two or three months' time was not worth the risk I had assumed.

It was two o'clock in the morning. Periods of blinding driving rain. The seas tore down and struck us almost abeam, each one larger than the last. Still, this was nothing, a mere summer's afternoon sail on Long Island Sound, compared to what it would be like in twelve hours if we did not get out of the path of the real hurricane itself. We were so far just skirting the edge of the winds of great violence, but feeling the strength of the storm in those tremendous seas that came not from the direction of the wind, but from the main centre of the tempest itself. . . .

Two o'clock in the morning — in a small floating fabric of wood and canvas — thrown first high on a crest, then tumbling deep in a trough. And two that I loved shut up below. And why? I asked myself. Why?

A slit of yellow light as the hatch is thrown back a bit to report on the barometer . . . still falling. That barometer — the major topic of thought for all three. On all sides of the hurricane the barometric pressure diminishes steadily toward the centre. As long as our glass fell it meant that the centre of the storm was approaching faster than we were side-stepping it. The hatch is quickly shut again. Some instinct warns me. I dive flat on deck and wrap myself around a stanchion. A smother of green phosphorescence sweeps over me, followed by solid water in a mighty roar as the Caribbean itself tries to swallow the tiny *Svaap*. She swims back from under the sea, pulls herself up from her beam ends, and staggers on minus the stays'l now but still carrying jib and mizen. Even this verged on insanity in such weather — but we were staking everything on driving ourselves out of it.

When she went over before the sea, there was pandemonium below. Everything in her must have gone on the loose. A few minutes of quiet and then hammering, faint below the closed hatch. What had happened . . . had she sprung a plank . . . was the water coming in? . . .

The hatch remained shut for a long while and the hammering went on. I could not leave the wheel. Later, the hatch slid open a few inches between seas — Dan's voice — full of awe — telling me that the big sea had torn the port berth (with Florence in it) and all the lockers beneath it loose from the hull. Cases of canned meat and butter and milk sprayed the cabin. The weight of these things, stored in the lockers beneath the berth, had supplied the inertia which, impelled by the force of the sea, had done the damage. It was fixed now temporarily. What was the barometer doing? Still falling? God! How are things on deck? Everything swell . . . she's going like hell, seas aren't any worse (you liar, you) . . . nothing to worry about, tell Florence that . . . been through much worse than this . . . Look out! Slam goes the hatch. Down crashes the sea on top of it. The warm torrent pours down on my head and over my body, leaving pulsating globs of green light all over me so that I look like the devil incarnate. I pull some gulf weed out of my hair and take a look to see if our two remaining sails are still hanging on. The hours drag — we fling on and on in a black and green void, counting off slow mile after mile, hoping that each one was one mile farther from the central maelstrom of the storm. But not knowing. Not knowing for sure until dawn had come — and noon — and afternoon again — when at last the rise of the barometer and the lengthening out of the seas told us we had won our race.

With a suddenness that was astonishing we ran out of the storm area and saw the blue sky and the sun. I took sights and found that we were just two hundred miles out. We had nothing further to fear. The great load of responsibility lifted from me, and the shadows of worry which the other two had tried so hard to keep me from noticing were gone. Everyone was all laughter (a bit too loud and ready at first, as the realization that we had won was slowly sinking in). We went overboard for the first swim for a long time, to tow on the end of a rope in the surging frothy wake. In a few hours we had forgotten the cyclone sweeping on relentlessly back there. It no longer affected us although we could still see on the horizon astern the dark mass of the hurricane cloud. With the amazing facility of sailors we had already forgotten all that agony of soul, the physical and mental strain we had been through, and drank in the beauty of an extravagantly coloured sunset while we ate a good supper on deck, all three of us. How good it was to be at sea — what other life could possibly compare with it!

We settled down to a comfortable voyage to Panama. When dawn came a few days later we saw the rain-shrouded land of the Isthmus ahead. That afternoon we anchored once more at the Atlantic terminus of the great canal.

CHAPTER VI

TO THE DARIEN OF LIONEL WAFER

WE had left Panama several days before, were in Pacific waters at last, and were cruising along the shores of Pedro Gonzales in the Pearl Islands. It was a peaceful, lovely morning. We slipped along close to the palm-lined shores before a gentle breeze. A troop of small noisy green parrots darted erratically from tree to tree with the speed of a flight of arrows, keeping us company along the shore.

Out of the sky dropped a graceful seaplane, circled overhead, and landed close by in a cloud of colour-shot spray.

It was our friend Ralph Sexton of the Isthmian Airways, with our mail, fresh bread, and chocolates for Florence. Our bad angel had been dozing, and for several days since leaving Panama we had had delightful leisurely cruising. We seemed infinitely remote from civilization but the plane had flown out from Panama and found us in an hour or so.

Soon we were once more alone. With the freshening sea breeze we set sail and headed for Rey Island. This was to be our last stop before heading across the Gulf toward Darien, where Balboa once stood and gazed for the first time upon the great new sea. On my first voyage I had sailed to Darien and had seen the River Sambu belching its muddy waters into the great Bay of San Miguel. I had seen giant crocodiles, and long slender river canoes filled with loin-clothed Chola families coming down to Garachiné to trade their ivory nuts and plantains with Señor Muñoz, that genial white-haired patriarch of Garachiné. Señor Muñoz had lived for so many years in Garachiné, the only white man there, that it was hard to visualize him as the fiery revolutionist who had long ago come from Colombia at the head of eighty men to fight for freedom. Only twelve of his brave band had survived the fighting when independence was finally won. And now old Muñoz — nearing the end of his earthly span — looked out upon the world with his kind smiling eyes and watched over his village of blacks. I had promised him that some day before he died I should come back and visit him again. And then, I had always planned, I would follow the winding Sambu, up to the Indian country.

We rounded Point de Cocos, on the south side of Rey Island, and anchored one more night in the Pearl Islands. The long curve of lovely palm-lined beach swept in a crescent to form a perfect anchorage. There were two thatch huts and two unfriendly blacks, and quantities of coco-nuts. In the small surf on the beach a flock of pelicans were busy with their fishing, flopping into the water from aloft with grotesquely dishevelled abandon but rarely missing their fish. And then they would sit bobbing on the surface like celluloid toys, complacent and smug as only a pelican can be.

In preparation for the Sambu we took our mosquito nets ashore to overhaul them. There we spread them out on the beach, patching holes and weighting the edges with sand. An exquisite tropical sunset held us spellbound. Wild pigeons and noisy parrots in the trees kept us company. The sea breeze died. *Svaap* lay motionless upon the purple water and all our world was at peace.

When the sea breeze came in the next day we set sail. The low islands dropped behind. Soon, through the haze ahead, we could make out the first cloud-wrapped ranges of the Andes and the lowland of Darien.

The evil genius that was presiding over our destiny began to stir. This over-confident little ship had been too long neglected as it was. And now she had the impudence to come into Darien, that stronghold of his, where for four hundred years he had plagued the encroaching white man with so many ills, with fever, hunger, hostile Indians, and general misfortune, that even now Darien

is unchanged from that day when the brave band of Spaniards cut their evanescent trail across the Isthmus.

Late that afternoon we anchored a mile out in the bay off Garachiné. At low tide we should almost be able to walk ashore. It was another coincidence of dates, for exactly five years before to the hour, I had anchored *Svaap* in the same spot. Things were unchanged: the straggling thatch village standing there on its posts in the mud; the house of Muñoz built over the water on stilts, and the Chinese store of similar style; the yam and plantain gardens out at the back, stolen from the edge of the jungle. A village of mixtures mostly well on the black side, of Negro, Indian, Chinese, and the predominating Spanish-plus-? blend that is called Panamanian. A poor squalid village in a setting that was magnificent, with the vast teeming jungle crowding down from the backdrop of impenetrable mountains and valleys. It was the rainy season, and those great green hills were more than usually cloaked with dense grey rain-squalls and tenacious clinging clouds. The river refuse of the Sambu swept past us swiftly, even though the mouth was still five miles away.

A dugout took us to where the mudflats began. Florence and I removed our shoes and waded barefoot the rest of the way to shore through the inevitable mud. I hesitatingly came to the Muñoz door. Would he still be living, I wondered, and all of a sudden there he was, looking more than ever like some strange South American Santa Claus. And his wife too, and all their children. We made their house our headquarters and planned our Sambu trip.

There was, in the village, a Panamanian who called himself by the imposing name of Gabriel Val de la Mar and who claimed to be a river pilot for the Sambu. I engaged him for the journey and made preparations to start the following day. As we returned to the *Svaap*, the rain came down in such torrents that two men bailing with half calabashes were barely able to keep the big dugout afloat.

It is hard to give any idea of the way it rains in Darien. It is more like standing under a waterfall than anything else. During the rainy season these rains are not just of cloudburst duration, but have a permanency about them that brings on a feeling of despondency. It often rains in that devasting fashion for two, three, or more days and nights. The rivers rise ten or fifteen feet and flood the country. Since our experience in Darien I have read Lionel Wafer's account[1] of his struggles in Darien in 1681, when with William Dampier and a small band of hardy pirates he returned across the Isthmus from a buccaneering expedition on the west coast. The hardships these men underwent were almost inconceivable. Wafer, whose knee was injured, had dropped, with four others, behind the main body of men. They were held for a time

---

[1] *A New Voyage and Description of the Isthmus of America.* Lionel Wafer was in the buccaneering rendezvous off Darien (on the Atlantic side) where 400 men met and, on April 5, 1680, set out to march across the Isthmus to attack Santa Maria, a Spanish gold-washing station on the Pacific side. They later split under various leaders, some returning, some capturing Spanish craft in which they went plundering. William Dampier was one of the latter. Bartholomew Sharp was in command most of the time. They haunted all the regions we were to visit with the *Svaap*.

by Indians but were finally released and resumed their crossing of Darien.

The first three Days we march'd thro' nothing but Swamps, having great Rains, with much Thunder and Lightning; and lodg'd every Night under the dropping Trees, upon the cold Ground. The third Night we lodg'd on a small Hill, which by the next Morning was become an Island: For those great Rains had made such a Flood, that all the Land about it was cover'd deep with Water. All this while we had no Provision, except a handful of dry Maiz our Indian Guides gave us the first two Days: But this being spent, they returned home again, and left us to shift for ourselves.

At this Hill we remained the fourth Day; and on the fifth the Waters being abated, we set forward, steering North by a Pocket Compass, and marched till 6 a Clock at Night: At which time, we arrived at a River about 40 foot wide, and very deep. Here we found a Tree fallen cross the River, and so we believed our men had pass'd that way; therefore here we sat down, and consulted what course we should take.

They had various trials, crossing and recrossing rivers, losing one man who slipped from a tree-bridge. 'The stream hurried him out of sight in a moment, so that we concluded he was Drown'd.' They found him later, a quarter of a mile downstream, 'sitting on the Bank of the River; who, when we came to him, told us, that the violence of the Stream hurry'd him thither, and that being in an Eddy, he had time to consider where he was; and that

by the help of some Boughs that hung in the Water, he
got out. This Man had at this time 400 pieces of Eight
at his Back: He was a weakly Man, a Taylor by Trade.'
Later they camped on a small hill:

> where we gathered about a Cart-load of Wood, and
> made a Fire, intending to set out the next Morning.
> But not long after Sun-set, it fell a Raining as if
> Heaven and Earth would meet; which Storm was
> accompanied with horrid Claps of Thunder, and
> such flashes of Lightning, of a Sulpherous smell,
> that we were almost stifled in the open Air.
>
> Thus it continued till 12 a Clock at Night; when
> to our great Terror, we could hear the Rivers
> roaring on both sides of us; but 'twas so dark, that
> we could see nothing but the Fire we had made,
> except when a flash of Lightning came. Then we
> could see all over the Hill, and perceive the Water
> approaching us; which in less than half an hour
> carried away our Fire. This drove us all to our
> shifts, every Man seeking some means to save
> himself from the threatening Deluge. We also
> fought for small Trees to climb: For the place
> abounded with great Cotton Trees, of a prodigious
> bigness from the Root upward, and at least 40 or
> 50 foot clear without Branches, so that there was no
> climbing up them.
>
> For my own part, I was in a great Consternation,
> and running to save my Life, I very opportunely met
> with a large Cotton Tree, which by some accident, or
> thro' Age, was become rotten, and hollow on one
> side; having a hole in it at about the height of 4 foot
> from the ground. I immediately got up into it as well
> as I could: And in the Cavity I found a knob, which

served me for a Stool; and there I sat down almost Head and Heels together, not having room enough to stand or sit upright. In this Condition I sat wishing for Day: But being fatigued with Travel, though very hungry withal, and cold, I fell asleep: But was soon awakened by the noise of great Trees which were brought down by the Flood; and came with such force against the Tree, that they made it shake.

When I awoke, I found my Knees in the Water, though the lowest part of my hollow Trunk was, as I said, 4 foot above the ground; and the Water was running as swift, as if 'twere in the middle of the River. The Night was still very dark, but only when the flashes of Lightning came: Which made it so dreadful and terrible, that I forgot my Hunger, and was wholly taken up with praying to God to spare my Life. While I was Praying and Meditating thus on my sad Condition, I saw the Morning Star appear, by which I knew that Day was at hand: This cheared my drooping Spirits, and in less than half an hour the Day began to dawn, the Rain and Lightning ceas'd, and the Waters abated, insomuch that by that time the Sun was up, the Water was gone off from my Tree.

Wafer finally found his companions — who had also perched in trees during the flood — and they resumed their weary way. Coming two hundred and fifty-two years after, we found his Darien unchanged, the floods still raging through the jungle with the same overwhelming unexpectedness.

CHAPTER VII

SAMBU PRELUDE

ALL that night the rain thundered on deck. All next morning it blotted out the land from our sight. We spread a sail and filled our tanks in five minutes. At noon it eased a bit and by one o'clock Gabriel Val de la Mar showed up, ready to go. The tide was high. We could cut straight across the flats for the river mouth. In an hour the jungle had closed in on us, as we followed the serpentine wanderings of the turbid yellow Sambu.

At first we made good time, for the still rising tide thrust back the river current. We wound our way through jungle so dense we could see no more than a few feet.

This was the real tropical jungle, the jungle one reads about and rarely finds — a dark dank swampy tangle of lianas and creepers, parasitic growths of all descriptions, enormous-leaved plants and ferns, all grown together into a single impenetrable mass. Enormous flowering plants blazing with colour hung their great blossoms out over the river. A fortune in orchids lay spread before us.

As the current increased with the miles we began to see gigantic grey trunks rearing into the sky an astonishing distance above the average roof of the jungle, with only a single burst of foliage at the very top. They were the mightiest trees I have ever seen. It was something worth coming for — this Darien jungle!

Toward evening, winding nearer and nearer the mountains, struggling against an ever stronger current, we began to pass occasional Indian huts with plantain and banana gardens. We passed several canoes, hugging the wall of the jungle to escape the worst of the current. We rounded a hairpin curve and came upon a tremendous sea-canoe, a vessel capable of voyaging to Panama with several tons of plantains. It was a dugout, hewn from one of those tremendous trees we saw, perhaps fifty feet in length and six or seven in width. She was heavily loaded, bound downstream. We overtook a venerable grey-bearded patriarch with his family, struggling upstream in a small dugout, and took them in tow. They grinned broadly at this unheard-of luck and puffed their pipes.

The current reached dangerous proportions. We

narrowly missed several large tree trunks driving down-stream like battering rams. Slowly we gained, and just at dusk reached a sharp bend round an island. Here the current became rapids — the end of navigation. We would go on from here in canoes to the Indian villages.

We anchored in a deadwater behind the island just as the rain came down again in earnest. A single thatch hut stood ashore, with a solitary jovial black inhabitant. Gabriel of the imposing name went ashore to bunk with him. We spread our mosquito nets over the ventilators — everything else closed to the rain — and retired into the steaming inferno below.

Dan was cooking — bananas, rice, eggs, tinned beef. Chunks of coco-nut for dessert, topped off by anti-malarial quinine and a lime and rum. We tried to forget the heat below and made plans. We would go on up-river to-morrow, rain or no rain. It would probably rain till doomsday. It fell in a steady roar on deck. Faintly through the din came the whistled minor notes of a single plaintive tune. It was our black resident ashore. Never in all his waking hours — and, since we stayed several days, we saw a good deal of him — did he cease the whistling of that solitary tune, except to speak or to eat. Far into the night, as we tossed in the heat, we could hear the faint melody. I doubt if he slept at all.

By morning the river had risen six feet and was moun-ting steadily. We peered out through a curtain of water at a watery world. The whistler's poor horse stood dejectedly beside the hut, belly deep in water, morosely

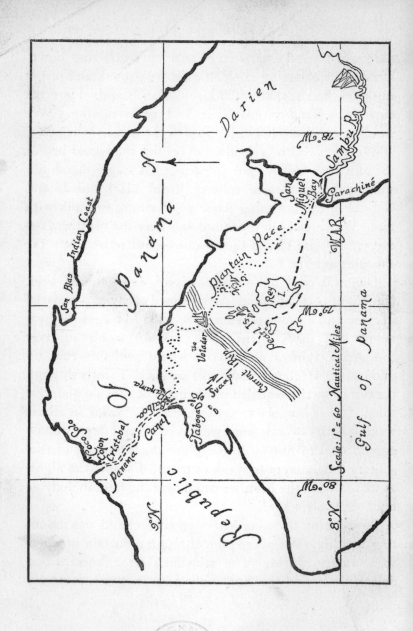

Darien

Panama

San Blas Indian Coast

San Miguel Bay

Sambu R.

Garachiné

78°W.

Plantain Race

Rey I.

Pearl Islands

Current Rip

the Volador

Otoque

Taboga

Republic Of

Panama

Balboa

Panama Canal

Cristobal

Colon

Chagres R.

79°W.

Gulf of Panama

Scale: 1"= 60 Nautical Miles

80°W.

9°N.

8°N.

munching some leaves that hung near its head. The pigs and the dog shared a platform a little distance from the house, loudly wailing their woes. Both structures were on posts, still out of reach of the muddy waters. Gabriel was not in sight, but on the platform sat a black figure, whistling his melancholy dirge.

In the whistler's long river *cayuca* we went upstream through the rain. The whole land was flooded. Where the river doubled back on itself in a figure S we saved miles by paddling straight across the land, for here the jungle was not so dense. Our devious progress, dodging the worst of the rapid-like current, finally brought us to the village of Pueblo Nuevo. To our great astonishment it was not an Indian settlement at all, but one of blacks.

The water raced through the village, nearly up to the springy split-bamboo floors. The dogs clung uncared-for to beams or low branches. From each front door trailed a long cayuca, tailing down with the current. They were lashed end to end to serve as thoroughfares and one could traverse the village by this precarious twelve-inch-wide canoe walk.

We stayed in Pueblo Nuevo for some time and then consulted Gabriel as to the Indian villages. He seemed very vague. I had already felt serious doubts about my Gabriel of the shifty eyes, and now knew that he had never been beyond the island where we were anchored. Whistler, however, explained that the Indian villages began ten miles beyond. We should have to start early the following day with fast Indian paddlers. He would arrange for them.

We shot downstream through the flooded country, cutting into banana plantings and sections of forest, and soon were back aboard *Svaap*. The never ending dirge-like whistling was beginning to tell on us, as was the rain which still fell in torrents. The Sambu was by now higher than ever — almost to the shoulders of the horse who seemed to take it as an unhappy but necessary situation. Again the rain fell all night in a steady unbroken torrent, and the flood rushed on.

At dawn our Indian paddlers were on hand, their glistening bodies streaming with water. They had a very long, very narrow dugout. We put our provisions and camera into a big airtight tin and were off. Again we forged upstream. It was different this time, for these men were superb paddlers, untiring, knowing all the flood-water short cuts, and the best places to avoid the current. At last we reached the Indian settlements. These were friendly Cholas, but completely primitive. A little distance beyond lay the land of the war-like Indians who keep out strangers. I had hoped to make contact with them, but with the river in this condition it was out of the question.

So we stayed where we were and became acquainted with the Cholas. We had a meal, opening tins of beef and producing hardtack, butter, and chocolate. They offered us a large cooked iguana, and flung a child's pet turtle into the red hot coals with the callous disregard of animal suffering common to savages. The cries of the child and the frantic scramblings of the turtle (which had to be pushed back into the fireplace once or twice) soon ceased. And so we ate — squatting on our haunches with them — and learned what we could of the life of these little known savages. Night caught us on the way back to *Svaap*, but our naked paddlers with their cat's eyes took us down through the rapids in safety.

CHAPTER VIII

REVENGE OF AN EVIL GENIUS

IT came when least expected, as these things do, and with lightning-like rapidity. We were under way again in *Svaap*, moving downstream to another anchorage by an isolated Indian habitation. The flood waters still raced through the country unabated, but the rain had at last slackened. Gabriel was steering for the anchorage. Just below, the river made a hairpin turn. The waters were so high that the current divided, part of it following the regular river bed, part cutting across through the jungle to rejoin the main stream below.

The current swung the bow off a bit. Gabriel suddenly lost his head and threw the wheel the wrong way. We shot broadside to, into the branch current, out of control. I was forward at the anchor. I leaped aft, but too late. Full speed we plunged straight into the wall of the jungle, crashed through bow first for about fifty feet, miraculously missing trees and carrying with us a mass of vines and foliage until we finally grounded. The current threw its full weight upon us and we heeled over on our beam ends, our masts entangled in a mass of branches. The disturbed birds of the forest screamed at the intrusion. A big lizard, vivid green, scrambled hastily away in the branches overhead to join the monkeys who had already left. The roar of the flood through the jungle was the voice of our evil genius, chuckling at his master stroke. It was like a waterfall, beating upon my consciousness with dull painful reiteration: '*Svaap* is Lost! Lost! Lost!'

There was nothing to say. Gabriel? Gabriel of the shifty eyes — sitting unconcerned there on the rail with his stiff straw hat shoved back on his head? Curse him? Revile him? Beat him to a pulp? Oh — but that would not bring *Svaap* back out of the jungle — that would not tear her loose from those parasite creepers that were already fastening their tentacles upon her lofty masts.

The world was very black indeed, just then, and just then Gabriel spoke, I think the first words that anyone had uttered.

'Señor! If we go on straight through there,' he pointed to the dense flooded jungle ahead, 'we get quickly to the river mouth.'

I don't think it was intended as humour — it was

scarcely the time or place for it — but the remark broke the tension. I took stock. The tide? Well, thought Gabriel, it is low now. At evening it will rise, perhaps six feet. So far upstream as this? Without doubt, Gabriel believed.

Then there was a chance. The Indian we had intended to visit arrived by canoe, expressing no surprise or emotion whatever. One might have thought ocean-going ketches were in the habit of ploughing through his back-yard jungle every day. I rushed him off up-river for reinforcements to try to get her out when the tide rose in the evening. We set about cutting the rigging free. After a two-hour struggle we got a line out astern where we had come from and across the racing river to a tree.

Night fell — but no rise in the tide — no abating of the mighty flood that was grinding us relentlessly deeper into the woods. We sat forlorn and quiet.

Suddenly through the dark we heard a jumble of excited voices. A long slender cayuca shot through the opening we had ploughed into the jungle and came along-side. The flickering yellow rays of our lantern fell on the wet naked bodies and grotesque faces of fifteen men, a motley mixture of blacks and Indians. Inky blackness everywhere except our little circle of flickering light. The constant undertone of the floodwaters. Shouted orders. Excited jumble of response out of the dark. The whole gang hauling at our end of the hawser. A fight to get across the river without losing our grip on the line. Groping for a foothold on the other side, a

Svaap is wrecked

band of pygmies in a maze of gigantic weeds and ferns, waist deep in clutching water. Then more sweating and hauling in the darkness from that end of the line.

The river fell instead of rising. *Svaap* was hard and fast. All that man-power was useless. Rum was passed around and flung down gaping throats. When a savage drinks, he pours down powerful spirits as a thirsty man might toss off a glass of cold water. We could hear their shouting and singing fade upstream, and blend with the moaning of the flood. What now? Try to sleep. Perhaps the river will rise in the morning as they say it will. . .

CHAPTER IX

RETURN TO GARACHINÉ

THE river was falling remorselessly. The natives returned in the morning but it was no use. I dealt out drink, sugar, biscuit, and sent them away. The rains had ended. The dry season was at hand. The river would return to its confines. *Svaap* was uninjured but in twenty-four hours she would be far from the nearest water. The monkeys and the parrots would soon play in her rigging.

There was only one chance: return to Panama for salvage equipment and hurry back. We could try to jack her up, build a skidway under her and move her ten tons of deadweight back out of the bush and into the river. It would be an engineering feat but we could try it.

I put it up to Florence and Dan. Were they willing to try it? Of course. They were game. Dan would have to stay and hold the fort. Otherwise the natives would return and strip the *Svaap*. The decision was made. Fifteen minutes after the men went upstream, we shot off down the Sambu, Florence and I, cramped in a small river cayuca with two Indians and Gabriel. Beyond Garachiné we had no plans, except that somehow we must get back to Panama, a hundred mile voyage from the river mouth. Dan looked very solemn as we left him there, alone in the Darien jungle with the forlorn wreck of the *Svaap*. There was no telling when he would see us again. The responsibility for him weighed heavily upon me as the dugout bore us round a bend and we could see him no longer.

Our equipment was scanty. Dan would need all the food that was aboard, so we took only a tin of beef, a half dozen hard biscuits, and a coco-nut. This would have to last us to Garachiné. We took also a bottle of St. Julien and one of champagne we had been hoarding for Christmas and New Year's Day. We had no clothes except what we wore. A blanket apiece and one large mosquito net, toothbrushes and razor, revolver, and camera completed our equipment for the arduous journey ahead.

Silent with our thoughts we slipped swiftly downstream. The hated face of Gabriel faced us in the stern.

I know now that he was never a pilot at all. I had felt
doubts when I first met him. If only I had followed
my better judgment . . . And local knowledge, I had
found, was all wrong . . . the tide would rise and hold
back the current they had said, first in the evening, then
in the morning. It fell instead, and the current abated
not a bit. Never put faith in anyone else's judgment
against your own in your own field of knowledge. Pilot
your own ship, as you would your ship of life.

We sat on knobby lengths of sugar cane to keep us out
of the water which constantly leaked in. Florence
leaned back against me and slept for a while. What a
terrific adventure this was going to be for her. And
through all the hardships never a complaint, but a rich
ability to see the amusing aspect when things were
dreariest.

All day the river fell. During the night we came to
Garachiné where we were taken in by kindly old Señor
Muñoz and his family.

We were lucky. Anchored out off the mudflats was
a large sailing dugout like the one we had met up the
Sambu. It was a single log, with built-up sides and
deck, and was perhaps 35 feet long and 6 feet wide.
It had two rickety masts, schooner rigged. Its name was
Volador and it belonged to Muñoz. He was even then
loading it with plantains for a voyage to Panama. She
would leave in a day or so.

When Muñoz learned what had happened he ordered

The Author starting down the Sambu after the wreck

the *Volador* to sail early the following morning. His other boat, the *Roma*, an old cutter with an engine, was somewhere on the coast also, gathering a cargo of plantains. She too would be going to Panama. We would have two or three days' start on her but with her engine she might catch us. It would be a race to reach Panama and get the best price for the plantains.

All night they poured the plantains into the *Volador* while we slept a few hours in camp beds set up in the Muñoz parlour. There should be an eternity of sweet reward waiting for this gentle old man and his open-hearted wife for their lives of simple charity and kindness toward their fellow men. Señora Muñoz mothered half the children of the village regardless of colour, bringing them up with her own without discrimination. The youngest of them gathered round the doors that night, very black in their white nighties, and in hushed excitement studied our every move as we prepared for bed, not leaving until we were finally tucked in.

We were wakened at two a.m. the following morning, November 5th, 1933, ready to board the *Volador*. Old Señor Muñoz padded around in his voluminous white nightshirt collecting coco-nuts for us and helping to get us started. We waded out over the mudflats to a cayuca and went aboard. The plantains were all there, and the passengers (being Florence and myself at two dollars apiece for the entire voyage, food included), but there was no sign of captain or crew. At four a.m. they arrived: the captain, the cook, and the slave. It was just getting light in the east when we lifted our tattered sails to the early morning land breeze.

I had always wanted to make a voyage in one of these large decked dugouts, relics of an almost forgotten age of primitive navigation, and so, even with the ever-present thought of *Svaap* and Dan back there in the jungle, it was a great adventure. Slowly we gathered way — and the Great Plantain Race of 1933 had begun.

CHAPTER X

THE GREAT PLANTAIN RACE

I<small>T</small> was an epic voyage. In the hold was a cargo of ten thousand curved green plantains from Darien. Amidships under a hatch a small space had been left among the plantains for us to crouch in when the rain came, as it surely would. This we shared with miscellaneous itinerant crabs, large spiders, and bilge water, for the craft leaked strenuously and needed hourly bailing.

We had enough coco-nuts so that we should not have to use the water on the *Volador*. Thus we had drink, and nourishment from the meat of the nut. These, and the bottle of champagne, were the only personal stores we brought along. The St. Julien had helped a little during the cramped discomfort of the down-river trip.

We stowed our coco-nuts and hung our luggage on a nail below decks, where neither rain nor bilge could reach it, and became acquainted with our shipmates.

The captain, a very unprepossessing black in ordinary shirt, trousers, and yellowed stiff straw hat (surely the world's least sea-going article), made one effort at the very start to impress us with the dignity of his position, calling the slave all the way aft in a loud voice to haul a line which lay at his very feet as he stood by the tiller. This done — his passengers sufficiently impressed with his importance — he relaxed into a sort of excess baggage for the duration of the trip. When the sun grew hot he would retire behind the mainsail to snore loud and long in its shade. When a rain squall came he would disappear into a hole up forward reserved for his sole use. When a storm came up one black night and his vessel was in danger, he firmly shut himself in his place of concealment up there and was not seen until morning when it was again fine weather.

The slave was a nondescript young negro, who never had a moment of peace, poor fellow. No sooner would he settle down for a nap than the helmsman would shout for him to slack off the sheets, to trim them in, to bring a drink, to bail out the bilge. He was so long-suffering that I felt really sorry for him. He could not even look forward to rest in port, for the good old *Volador* was leaking always.

The real character of the voyage was the cook-mate, Manuela, who should have lived three hundred years ago and sailed with Morgan the pirate. He could not help looking piratical. The remnants of his sombrero hung in tatters around his face. Boiling his fish and plantains, or steering the long afternoon watch — whatever he did — he always managed to get into picturesque attitudes. When the sun grew hot he would lie on the deck, head on the low rail, one arm around the tiller, entirely covered by a large grass sleeping mat. Dozing in this way, he would steer for hours without coming up for air. If the wind shifted, or the *Volador* got too far off course, I would poke him gently, and he would lift a heavy-lidded face out from under the mat. He was always cheerful and did what he could to make us comfortable.

The land breeze soon failed and we rolled in the swell until the sea breeze came in from the south-west. Then the old *Volador* gathered speed. I was delighted with the way she sailed. She stood up to the freshening breeze beautifully, with much more stability than I had expected. Her long cigar-shaped hull slipped along so easily that she left practically no wake at all.

We spread a blanket on the narrow deck and relaxed with the gentle pleasant motion. I remember counting the patches on the mainsail as I lay there. There were eighteen major ones, twelve of these patches themselves being repatched. There were hundreds of small holes and tears. I was wondering what would happen in a blow, when I fell asleep.

When I awoke we had raised the Pearl Islands on the port bow. At this rate we should be in Panama in twenty-four hours. The prospect cheered us so much that we pulled ourselves together and bathed as well as we could under the circumstances. I broke open a coconut. We used part of the liquid for brushing our teeth and then while I shaved with the remainder, Florence did her hair. We had been a pretty dreary pair before, but now, refreshed by sleep and washed, things seemed brighter and more hopeful.

An hour or so before noon Manuela prepared to get a meal together. The galley consisted of a fireplace on deck, just forward of the mainmast. There was soon a mess of rice boiling over a cheerful little fire. The rice was really delicious. It was made with fresh milk which Manuela squeezed from the rich white meat of a coconut. The rice put to one side, he applied himself to the preparation of a sort of Panamanian *bouillabaisse* consisting of plantains and fish (heads, bones and all) boiled down to a thick soup. This was pretty awful, more than we could go, so we had roasted plantains instead. This was our regular diet for the trip — rice and plantains, plus the milk and meat of the coco-nuts we had brought with us. Rice, as cooked by the Panamanian, becomes a wonderfully appetizing and satisfying dish, far different from the soggy mess that is met with elsewhere. We are both as fond of plantains now as we were before the start of the Plantain Race when they became a constant diet three times a day every day.

That day passed peacefully. Night fell and a bright moon shone. We lay down to sleep in the only possible place, just aft of the mainmast, on deck. It was hard but we were tired and slept until suddenly the boom, which only cleared the deck by inches, swept across nearly rolling us into the sea. We scrambled around to the other side and resumed our rest, but only temporarily, for the breeze had changed, was squally and constantly shifting so that we were forced to tack. Then the rain came, in torrents, and drove us to share the hold with the plantains, the crabs, and the spiders. For Florence, who has a dread of spiders, this was nothing less than sheer heroism. The hatch cover was pulled shut over us and we were in complete inky blackness.

We perched on a low shelf just clear of the bilge water. The shelf was again bumpy sugar cane stalks, upon which we had reclined all the way down the Sambu. I know of very few things more uncomfortable. There was not enough room to stretch out or to sit upright, so after the fashion of savages we squatted there leaning against the plantains and tried not to get pitched into the bilge. The water rushed noisily back and forth, splashing us occasionally. When it got too high we shouted for the slave to come and pitch some of it out with a five-gallon tin.

The motion became violent — we heard wind — and shouts on deck as the sails came down. A bad squall, for which the Gulf of Panama is famous, had hit us. The turmoil lasted for some time and then I felt the

Volador getting under way again as the storm abated. Our black pit heeled far over and stayed there. The rain still pounded overhead unceasingly. The sea rushed noisily past our slender hull as it leaped vibrating through the waves. This was great, we thought, we'd be in Panama to-morrow.

Just then the hatch was opened a little and a voice came down through the blackness — the voice of Manuela.

'Señor — please come!' There was an urgency in his tone so I threw off my clothes to keep them dry and crawled out, abandoning Florence to the mercy of the spiders and crabs.

Outside was nearly as black as below — only a yellow glimmer from the binnacle box by the helmsman. This binnacle box was a wonderful contraption, built exactly like a small dog kennel which we took it to be at first. In one side stood a rusty Dietz lantern and opposite was the compass, an ancient affair with card so dim it could hardly be read.

The *Volador* was footing it fast under fore and stays'l. Manuela and the slave, water pouring off them in streams, were huddled together by the tiller, jabbering in Spanish. They seemed very much confused and a little frightened. They knew the course was north-west but they were befuddled with the compass. The captain was shut up in his retreat on account of the storm. Could I show them?

I looked at the compass. The box had been shoved to one side to make room for their feet and the centre line was at least forty-five degrees from the fore and aft line of the boat. Yet they were trying to steer by it. I straightened the thing — they could not see why — and wedged it in place with some timbers. I showed them which was north-west and stood by for a while until I was sure they were holding the course. Then I rejoined Florence below with the plantains, where we perched like a pair of leghorns until morning brought sunshine and release.

This day was unbelievable. We were several miles off Pacheca Island when the breeze died that morning at sunrise. Ahead lay an endless undulating line of flotsam, refuse from the recent floods in Darien rivers. Converging current had marshalled it into a solid narrow belt and it swept on out to sea.

The captain, sensing the return of fine weather from the depths of his retreat, slowly emerged blinking in the sudden light. His eyes lit, after a moment, on the near-by stream of rubbish. A wide smile wreathed his black features. Here was manna from Heaven. He took the tiller. We still had a breath of wind — enough to get farther away from that mess before we became really becalmed — and that is what I thought he was going to do at first. With amazement we watched him steer directly for it, where we at once became entangled with the branches of a large floating tree. Pushing into the very centre of the mess, they lowered sail and spent the entire day fishing out miscellaneous rubbish from the steady stream which drifted past. There were coco-nuts galore, unspoiled by immersion. These were a welcome addition to our diminishing larder. They collected perhaps a half cord of firewood for the galley — the slave being relegated to the plebeian task of chopping it up while they had the fun of fishing it out. A packing-case cover floated alongside and just fitted the stove as a cover. A dead pig drifted along, but they had the strength of character to resist it. There were chickens, iguanas, seagulls, many more — in that procession of the dead. All day long this stream of Darien offal drifted past and we lay and cooked in the sun.

Meanwhile the current carried us remorsely miles out to sea, and the hills of the mainland faded from sight. Several times we sighted small vessels, hull down, heading for Panama, and conjectured as to which might be the *Roma*. With her engine she would surely beat us now.

Finally, in the evening, a light wind came in out of the west and we again started off toward Panama, but not without longing looks back at the sinuous stream winding its way out into the sunset across the gulf.

Another night and another day. Then we were almost there. All the last night we could see the beacons of Balboa reaching out their guiding rays to us. It was a magnificent night. We were close to the coast with a light land breeze that smelled of the jungle. All night we tacked at half hour intervals. Each time Florence and I would pick ourselves wearily up and climb around to the other side of the deck to escape the boom. Then we were again becalmed.

Mid morning — one of those intensely blue mornings you get on the Pacific, and sometimes on the Mediterranean — brought a faint sea breeze which slowly drifted us into Panama Bay, and there we left the *Volador* and its trusty crew of three. The *Roma* was not yet in. Our noble *Volador*, somewhat water-logged, had won the Great Plantain Race of 1933.

As a bum-boat carried us shoreward, we saw the captain relax for a nap in the shade of the draped mainsail and Manuela starting to cook his rice. The slave set to bailing resignedly.

CHAPTER XI

RETURN TO DARIEN

For days we had lived cramped in a native dugout, eating plantains and rice and coco-nuts. From far up the Sambu in Darien we had come to Panama by river and by sea in this primitive fashion to find equipment to salvage the *Svaap*, stranded in the jungle.

Now, in Panama at last, our first thought was for our personal rehabilitation. Into the dignified and conservative Hotel Tivoli we marched, Florence and I, in our shirts and shorts and sweaters. We were none too clean, unkempt from our strange voyage, our personal effects tied up in a red Tahitian *pareu*. It looked like the

bundles of washing one sees down there on top of
coloured mammies' heads. I scrawled in the register
and we rushed on to our room before the clerk had
recovered his composure enough to speak. And then
baths, long hot baths — new clothes — good food — long
undisturbed nights in a comfortable bed! Oh, what
luxuries these simple things become when one has lived
as we had of late.

But we were not to revel in these things for long. We
at once began a hectic week of preparation for the almost
impossible job that awaited us: the job of extracting the
Svaap from the clutches of the Darien jungle. Here and
there I collected two tons of salvage gear — timbers —
rollers — powerful lifting jacks — heavy cables and huge
double and triple blocks — picks, axes, shovels, machetes,
and tools. And there were food stores, and a quantity
of silver coins to pay the river natives for working.

Then the problem of a boat. That sounds simple
enough with all the small craft in Panama. But try to
get one the right size in a hurry. We wasted precious
time on false promises that this boat and that boat would
be in from a trip to-morrow and then be available.
Always to-morrow, *Mañana*. And then old Señor
Muñoz's ancient *Roma* came creeping in one day from
Garachiné with her load of plantains. Our fate seemed
tied for the time being to old white-haired Muñoz.
This has often happened to me in my wanderings.
Somewhere, unplanned, I share an experience with
someone. We part presumably for good, only to be

thrown in contact again and again until the fated series of events has run its course and the chapter closes. Thus with old Muñoz — who came benignly on the scene five years ago, to return again and again, almost indispensable, during our present depressing adventure.

The *Roma* was not a dugout like the *Volador*. She was a leaky little thirty-five-foot cutter with an ancient single-cylinder engine. We fell upon her captain like one of those Gulf squalls he knew so well, and chartered her before he knew what had happened.

Then, before we started, Ralph Sexton flew us down to Darien one day to make sure of the conditions that now existed on the Sambu. Out over the Pacific we flew, through the snowdrifts of the early morning clouds. Then out of the clouds over the Pearl Islands — rich green pearls they were, with shimmering emerald shoals and reefs — in a sapphire setting. Then on over the sea toward the Gulf of San Miguel. There lay the little village of Garachiné sleeping on its mud-flats. And the mouth of the Sambu. We roared over the jungle, climbed over cloud-wrapped mountains and searched for the familiar curves of the upper river. *Svaap* lay on her side, her sails up to dry, in a little clearing near the bank of the still receding river. Trees had been felled during our absence. Upstream stood the Indian house in another small clearing. Everywhere else, as far as one could see, stretched the mighty Darien jungle.

Dan and another figure, the Indian, stood by the *Svaap*. The river was too tortuous to risk a landing so

Svaap lies in the Jungle

we swung low over the treetops a few times, signalled to Dan, and again headed for Panama. We were back for lunch, thinking of those long days and nights we had spent covering half the distance in the *Volador*.

Our two tons of gear lay on the dock in Balboa. Then we discovered that the Balboa Port captain would not permit the *Roma* (unlicensed for Canal Zone waters) to come to the dock to load our gear. No exception would be made even in our extremity, so it was necessary to load our things first aboard a Canal Zone boat and rendezvous with the *Roma* outside, transhipping our cargo at sea. This was just a minor example of the unwillingness of the Balboa authorities to co-operate with us or make things easy.

Thus it was almost night when we finally got under way on the *Roma*. We had a dozen passengers, black and Indian, of assorted sexes and ages ranging from one new-born babe to an aged hag going back to end her days in Garachiné after seventy years absence. Why anyone in the world should want to go back to Garachiné to end their days is inconceivable.

There was no cabin — just a big cargo hold and the captain's cramped hole up forward with a bare platform to sleep on. This was set aside for our use. The passengers stayed on deck except when it rained. Then they crawled down with the cargo. One man — wasted almost to a skeleton — lay there always, on a coil of our big hawser. No one paid the slightest attention to him, although he was delirious most of the time, vomiting black. I discovered the second day that he was dying of blackwater fever. Our quinine seemed to help him to some extent and he was stronger and pathetically grateful when he was carried off at Garachiné.

The first night a violent squall hit us, blowing the mainsail to pieces. The little eight-horse-power engine carried on valiantly, aided by the jib. Our sleep was fitful. We seemed to be on a direct line between the rat headquarters up forward and the supplies aft, and were converted into an arterial highway by the rodents who had no compunctions about walking on our bodies. When the rat traffic slowed up, the cockroaches marched on — lovely big shiny brown ones two or three inches long. A Panamanian sea-going cockroach is a formidable creature. He can fly like a swallow and reproduce like a super guinea-pig. Elsewhere I have told my story of one of these creatures springing a rat trap and getting caught in it. This actually happened upon the *Svaap*. The crews of native boats like the *Roma* often wake from sleep to find the thick calloused soles of their feet being eaten by the cockroaches.

The second morning at two a.m. (it was November 17th) we arrived off Garachiné. A little later we went ashore, over the mudflats, to the house of Señor Muñoz.

Inconceivable news awaited us. Indians coming down-river had reported that *Svaap* was now safely anchored in mid-river. We were weak with joy. The impossible had happened. Some new flood, pushed back by a freak tide, had allowed them to refloat the ketch and extricate her from the jungle. But how? I still could not believe it . . . but it was so.

I had brought from Panama a native carpenter of sorts, with all his tools, to repair possible damage to *Svaap*. He was now superfluous. We left him with all his equipment in Garachiné to return to Panama, while we hurried on up the river in the *Roma*, now rid of her passengers.

We found the river in medium flood stage and crept along all day against an ever-increasing current — with equally increasing excitement. The parrots and snowy egrets kept us company. The evening was one of beautiful lights and reflections, and joy in our hearts. Night fell and we laboured on by the light of the stars. Night on the jungle river. . . . On into the white mist-mantled hills. Hours of suspense wondering how Dan and the *Svaap* were. The slow put-put-put of the engine re-echoed through the hills. Our hearts beat almost as loud. The old *Roma* — we had long ago added an A to make it *Aroma* — could barely do the last mile or so. It was nearing midnight. At each bend we would whisper — around the corner lies *Svaap*.

Finally we did come to the narrow neck of land that separated us from the scene of *Svaap's* stranding. The last of the interminable serpentine curves lay ahead. A tiny yellow light flickered for a moment through a hole in the jungle. . . . We would soon be aboard again with our own clean comforts . . . no more rats cavorting over us in the night . . . what a godsend that the *Svaap* had been floated out of the jungle. . . .

The last curve stopped us — a huge tree-trunk caught at the bend narrowed the channel to dangerous proportions. We groped against the rushing current, lost ground, gained, then entered the home stretch with the engine gasping out its heart against the stream. Foot by foot — inch by inch. Finally we reached the wide curve of slack water where *Svaap* should have been. The light shone yellow over the black water, beyond. There she was. We headed for the light and suddenly hit the bank with a soft bump. It was the dying fire of the Chola house we had seen, not the light of the *Svaap*. We backed off. Down there, faint against the black wall of the jungle, lay a white botch just where *Svaap* used to lie. Could it be? . . .

What terrible mistake was this? Had they cruelly fooled us or was this a horrible nightmare? We were closer now and the realization entered my brain like a slow-driven wedge that *Svaap* was not only where she had been, but she was wrecked. She was in a different position — strained — tortured — nearly keel up. She looked dismasted too. Our cries rang through the black stillness of the night.

'Dan . . . Oh, Dan . . .'

The *Roma* had anchored. Her engine was silent. There came a faint echo of our shouts from the jungle and a deathly silence. Even the night noises of the forest seemed to cease — everything but a little gurgle

88

of water rushing by the *Roma*. We were afraid to call again — afraid there would be no answer. It was a moment of eternity and then the eternity ended. A faint shout came from the Chola house — Dan's voice.

It was a scene I shall never forget although I have no recollection of getting ashore. Midnight in the Darien. We stood on the bank with the rushing river behind us. The long-haired Indian family roused themselves from their sleep and stood around us naked — the man and his two wives. Dan was almost inarticulate with grief as he tried to tell what had happened. Tears crept silently down Florence's cheeks.

Svaap had been refloated on a new flood with an extraordinary high tide that had backed up the current for a time. She had been anchored for an hour or so when the tide began to recede. The flood waters, with nothing to oppose them now, came down with greater fury than even the first time. *Svaap* was flung back into the clearing that had been made and thrown on top of the tree stumps which tore great holes in her. The river flowed through her for days. When the waters had finally abated she had crashed down with finality on to the stumps.

We picked our way with a lantern through a trail Dan had made and came to the wreck. She lay there, a thing in agony. Two of the tallest stumps, of great girth, pierced completely through the bottom on the starboard side and thrust the floor timbers out through the planking on the other side. She looked a total loss.

It is hard to give any idea of the feeling one can develop for an inanimate thing like a boat. We had lived together and sailed together for more than fifty thousand miles . . . seven years. It was like being present at the death of a loved one. For a moment I had no thought but that it was the end of her. Then I saw that she was not dismasted as I had feared. Her masts and rigging were intact. I examined the damage again, while Florence stood silently with Dan, waiting to hear what the decision would be. I experienced a strange sudden wave of defiance. 'Do it! Do it!' it said. 'Fight this evil genius, this jinx, to the wall and bring *Svaap* back to Panama if it takes the rest of the year. Rebuild her if necessary!'

The flood of determination swept through us all and we felt warm confidence that we could succeed against any odds.

Instant action was necessary, to catch the carpenter before he could leave Garachiné. We were going to need him and his tools now, more than we had ever dreamed. We picked our way back to the Chola house. It was like a pawn shop. Dan had moved everything over from the *Svaap* and stored it here, thinking *Svaap* was done for. I gave the *Roma* men instructions for the preliminary work. We took the Indian's slender cayuca and two paddlers from the *Roma* crew and started immediately downstream — Florence and I. It was the middle of the night.

At first stars. Then inky blackness down the miles of winding river. Occasionally we hit the bank or a snag.

Now and then the overhanging jungle would clutch at us and tear at our hair. Cold. Wet. Cramped. Finally rain. Twenty-five miles through the black jungle in a twelve-inch-wide dugout! The rushing river added to the swiftly ebbing tide flung us out of *La Boca* — the mouth — just before dawn. Then we followed the mangroves, not to get lost in the open Gulf. The paddlers were almost spent. A gleam of yellow light through thatch, where the night lights burned to keep away evil spirits, showed us where the village of Garaché lay sleeping. The east was beginning to grow grey. We ran the surf beside Muñoz's rambling house on piles.

It was only a small river canoe. A wave curled up under us. We were swamped, swimming about rescuing our possessions.

Oh, Darien! what a hellish place you are, composed of the elements of misfortune and disaster, haunted with tragedy in your steaming jungle and glowering mountains.

CHAPTER XII

JUNGLE SALVAGE

THE cocks crowed throughout the sleeping village and the dogs rushed at us. We stood forlornly dripping before the Muñoz door. It was the second time we had come to his door at the break of dawn, but our reception was warmer than ever. True hospitality is always prepared and, I fear, long-suffering. Without old Muñoz and his motherly wife we would have been homeless in Garachiné. Dan also would have been lost without his stoic, taciturn Chola Indian host.

After three hours' sleep our paddlers were ready to start again. I sent them off with Adams, the carpenter, and his gear, with instructions for starting the work. The *Roma* was sent orders to stand by. We stayed to get together additional material now needed for the salvage job.

We were in weird clothes, Florence in a shapeless faded dress of Señora Muñoz's, myself in Muñoz's capacious trousers. Our own things were drying. I again felt terribly low — completely defeated. The defiant confidence had leaked away during those miserable cramped rain-drenched night hours in the dugout. How could we possibly hope to do anything with the *Svaap* in that condition? Everything was black and hopeless.

Florence was miraculous, keeping her spirit throughout, never a complaint at all the hardship, thinking not of herself but of my well-being . . . such a man's woman as one might not find the world over. And the next day, when we again started up the river by canoe, our fifth traverse so far, she was as cheerful as ever. I had tried to make her stay in Panama. Her brother and sister-in-law were there for the winter, and we had many friends there. She could have comforts and luxuries. To come with me meant weeks of toil and hardship in the malarial Darien. She refused to be shelved in Panama however, and when the old *Roma* sailed she was aboard.

We had increased our quinine dose from nine grains to fifteen daily in view of possible exposure to the malarial Anopheles mosquito that night coming down the river when we had no nets. And so, as we turned up-river again, our ears were ringing although we were silent with our thoughts. I was planning the job that lay ahead. Ten tons of boat to be raised from the stumps, patched up well enough for a voyage to Panama, and moved bodily out to the river bank, and down the sheer ten foot drop of the bank itself. With our meagre and primitive equipment, and inexperienced help, it seemed an appalling job. I didn't dare to think what chance of success we had. And it was all so unnecessary. My instinct had told me when I hired him that Gabriel was not the man we wanted. Why I did it I can't say. I have always been somewhat psychic and rarely go wrong when I follow my instincts.

I am reminded of a strange thing that happened when we were in Panama getting together our salvage material. We were at the Tivoli. We went to bed one night at a fairly early hour. I was tired and fell asleep almost at once, only to awaken a little later full of terror. I could not explain it at all. I had not been dreaming and nothing had happened which might have produced this frame of mind. I turned on the lights and searched the room and bathroom. Back in bed, with a revolver under my pillow, I tossed and turned sleeplessly. I was still full of the most indescribable dread of something terrible that was going to happen, some awful impending danger about to strike at us from an unknown source. I remained awake, watchful, until morning came at last with nothing more eventful than a visit by a small grey mouse. . . . But up on the Sambu that night, my beloved

Svaap was thrown upon the stumps and wrecked. My night of terror had not been for nothing.

Our new paddlers were the best we had had, and we struck a favourable tide almost all the way up. We were getting used to travelling up and down the Sambu and the weary miles seemed to slip past more quickly this time.

The next morning the little jungle clearing became a hive of activity. I had twelve men in all, not counting ourselves. There were Chola Indians from near by, the native captain and crew of the *Roma*, and Adams the Panamanian carpenter. All except Adams worked cheerfully and hard to the end. The Indians were by far the best of all. Adams, coming from the Canal Zone and its high scale of wages, with his tools and supposed skill, was paid four dollars a day but was above soiling his hands by real labour. He did speak the native tongue, however, and made a good interpreter-foreman. Next came the engineer of the *Roma* at a dollar and a half a day and the captain at a dollar — which after all is just, I suppose, for without the engineer the captain would be worth nothing. The crew received seventy-five cents a day and the Indians about the same, except that they were partly paid in axes and other tools.

Florence and I slept under a single net on a hatch on the *Roma's* deck, surrounded by the entire crew. The Indians went home at night. Dan continued to sleep in the near-by Chola house where he had lived during our absence.

95

We all crowded aboard at mealtime and were fed by the cook of the *Roma*. Rice, plantains, tinned meat, and hardtack. All meals were approximately the same except breakfast when the tinned meat was omitted. We had a small stock of tinned things, from which we occasionally added to the simple fare, but for the most part we ate just what our men ate and we all ate together. It made for good feeling and co-operation.

Once started, the work progressed far better than I had hoped. Trenches were dug under the hull. Jacks were placed in these and the boat was slowly lifted about fifteen inches and blocked. The jacks were placed higher and the process repeated. In this way we had the *Svaap* blocked upright in a normal position by the end of the first day.

The next job was to repair the damage to the hull as well as we could with our limited material. She had fallen on her starboard side. Here, in two places down near the keel, her planking and frames had been crushed by tree stumps. On the port side opposite were two corresponding holes where the floor timbers had been forced all the way through by the stumps.

We cut out the planks as far as any damage extended and fitted in lengths of native mahogany I had found in Garachiné. Then all four patched areas were caulked, puttied, and painted. To make sure there were no leaks we tacked canvas over the patches with plenty of thick paint underneath. On top we tacked tin sheathing. We had no proper sheathing, but slit open empty five-gallon petrol tins and flattened them out. This served the purpose quite well.

Then came the difficult job — the skidway. The *Svaap* now stood in a position parallel with the river, about thirty feet from the bank, so we decided to launch her sideways. We had brought along from Panama timbers, eight inches square. To form the bed of the skidway we dug two long parallel trenches passing under the keel at the proper places. In them we set a pair of these timbers. Next we dug holes fore and aft under the keel for lifting-jacks. Then very slowly and carefully, inch by inch, we jacked the whole boat, blocking and all, until there was clearance enough under the keel for rollers and another set of identical timbers.

For rollers we had only two long sections of heavy iron piping about four inches in diameter. Two men working all day with hacksaws cut these into two-feet lengths. The jacks were eased off now until the keel rested across the top pair of beams. The blocking was then shifted so that it also rested upon these top beams, which became in effect a platform supporting the *Svaap* — the whole structure resting upon rollers which travelled upon the bottom beams. This had all been a very delicate job. A mistake anywhere would have sent the *Svaap* crashing down upon the workers. This work so far took four days.

Our whole life up there on the Sambu seemed strangely unreal. I have worked with boats in many strange places. I have beached the *Svaap* in the Galapagos and

careened her in the Solomons with woolly-haired canni-
bals watching from the bushes. But up there on the
Sambu was the strangest of all. Sometimes, during the
heat of the midday sun, we went to the Indian house,
clambered up the notched log that served as ladder to
the elevated floor, and sat among our worldly possessions.
A squaw crouched to one side weaving a new basket,
watching us surreptitiously, and particularly examining
Florence in every detail. A sickly baby, swinging in a
tiny hammock, fretted and cried. A larger child pulled
at the tail feathers of the much-pestered pet parrot. A
curl of smoke rose from the ever-present fire. This, for
three weeks, was Dan's home. When we returned to
work, picking our way through the denseness of the
jungle, it was always with amazement that we flung aside
the last veil of ferns and vines that hung across the
trail — and discovered *Svaap*, standing there among the
trees. From there no river could be seen, and the boat
looked as incongruous as a whale in the Sahara.

There was beauty up there on the Sambu — lush
colourful beauty of which we drank deeply in our rare
moments of ease. The early morning river had a character
of its own — with its white mist-mantle spread softly
everywhere, and mountains showing through above. At
slack water, when the swelling breath of the Pacific held
back for a time the five-knot current of the river, the
jungle leaned over and watched itself reflected in the
still waters. In the evening, our strenuous day's work
done, we rested on the deck of the *Roma*, drinking

coco-nut milk, while smoke rose curling from the open galley fire on deck. The violent greens of the Darien jungle would soften and absorb the sunset colours.

And so this night, with everything prepared and everything hingeing on the morrow, we ate our plantains and rice and beef, and hoped all would go as planned. By to-morrow night the *Svaap* would be floating there with the *Roma*. If our plans failed for getting her down that sheer ten-foot drop of the river bank, she would never sail again.

At dusk, after the long twilight, the Anopheles came out and we crawled beneath our net. Florence was as tired as I, for she was working too — from morning until night — with our things in the Chola house. When the bottom was smashed in by the stumps, the *Svaap* had filled with muddy river water and everything was in a terrible mess. Florence washed and rinsed and dried — stringing lines between the trees of the Indian clearing until the place looked like a Chinese laundry. There were guns and other equipment to be cleaned and oiled, and a hundred other things for her to do. And so we fell asleep almost the moment we relaxed, even though we were cramped together on a hard hatch cover, surrounded by our jabbering native crew.

We were up at dawn that eventful day. *Svaap* stood poised on her primitive marine railway. For power to move her forward we used the same jacks that had lifted her. We put in 'deadmen' — upright posts buried deep in the ground with only a little projecting above the surface. The jacks were butted horizontally against these posts, and as they were expanded they pushed against the upper beams that carried the *Svaap*. It worked beautifully although with some minor difficulties; the rollers tried to get off the track; one of the top beams worked sideways in spite of everything we did, so that we had to stop, jack up that whole end and re-align it. But by late afternoon we had moved the *Svaap* out of the jungle and as near the brink as we dared.

At this point a distant hum grew into a full-throated roar and Sexton's little blue seaplane swooped low over the tree tops. Three times she dived, each time dropping a little white bomb. Then she climbed and circled overhead.

Everyone went mad. The thrill of such a visit from another world was almost too much for us. We poor exiles shouted and leaped after the little white bombs. One overshot and landed in the jungle. Another was close, falling into the bush at the edge of the clearing. We dived into the thick tangle regardless of thorns and insects. Others piled into canoes and tore after the third which fell in the river. We found them both. They were messages saying that our friends in Panama were worried. If the men in the plane saw that we were in difficulties a relief expedition would be sent to us. We devoured the messages which were duplicates. The plane came low again and we gave the signal that everything was all right. They could see that the *Svaap* was ready to be launched.

Relaunching *Svaap*.

They circled again and flew off in the direction of Panama.

This was the third time a plane had flown out from Panama to *Svaap*.

We were now ready for the big gamble. *Svaap* stood on the top of a sheer ten foot drop. The ends of the track beams extended out into mid-air. On their inner ends rested *Svaap*, on its movable platform. The bank was of soft earth and mud, bound together by a net-work of roots. Ten tons of boat rested on the very edge of the bank. We chopped loose some of the roots holding the bank together. The edge began to cave in slowly under the heavy pressure. We pushed an inch or so more with the jacks and our beams began to tip down more and more as the bank slowly collapsed. We had a heavy cable around the boat and to a tree behind, to hold her back. She was blocked so that she leaned in toward the forest. When the skids started to tip over the edge she came to more nearly an upright position. She must not tip over the other way or she would be lost.

We slacked a little on the cable. She stood hesitating a moment and then took the plunge. The beams tipped down until their ends hit the bottom. The *Svaap* slid down in a wild mighty rush and disappeared over the brink. The soft mud of the river bottom received her keel and there she rested — uninjured. It was a moment of great relief to all, for it had been a risky business. We had gambled and won. Our evil genius had lost a round.

The river rose a few feet at sunset. *Svaap* was now

almost afloat. We made levers of twenty-foot timbers and exerted enormous force against the stern. She came loose suddenly — and slid out into the stream, swaying gracefully to find her balance, in her own element once more after three weeks among the trees.

Our herculean task was done. We again walked the deck of *Svaap*, though it seemed unfamiliar after the *Volador* and the *Roma*. Next day we cleaned the mud-mantle from her. The river had been running right through her and had left the good old Sambu mud inside and out. Then, while I paid off the Indians, Florence and Dan ferried our gear out from the Chola house and dumped it all below. Our engine had been submerged and was out of commission. The *Roma* got under way with us in tow and for the eighth time we saw the winding miles of the Sambu creep past. We put our things in order. We bent on the sails in preparation for the sea. The magnificent jungle slipped past, unnoticed. We felt we knew the river by heart. Six times we had traversed its length by water, and we had flown up and down by plane. Florence sighed with relief — as we all did — when we had left the river mouth behind for the last time. She had been quite sure, she confessed, that she was doomed to spend the rest of her life going up and down the Sambu. We had all been pretty positive *Svaap* would never feel the lift of salt water again.

We stopped at Garachiné to pay the *Roma* bill and say farewell to old Muñoz. We were completely out of supplies, so we bought dozens of eggs, ripe plantains and green ones, drinking coco-nuts and riper ones for their juicy meat, yams, native rice, and oranges. We were completely native by now and these supplies seemed food for the gods.

We also bought a dugout canoe to replace our 'Fold-flat' row-boat which had served long and well, but was lost in the flood. This was our only small boat for the remainder of the voyage.

The season was nearing an end. Already it was blowing a cold nor'wester instead of the balmy south-west winds we had had before. Our sails thundered overhead as we waved farewell to Garachiné for the last time and settled down to our long beat of a hundred miles to Panama.

CHAPTER XIII

A THOUSAND MILES SOUTH

THE study of ocean currents is one of the most enchanting subjects I know. Hand in hand with the prevailing winds of the great seas they have guided, even controlled through the centuries, the spread of exploration and human knowledge. Much more important than the winds, though, the great ocean currents control climates themselves, and thus the habitability and fertility of great regions. The Gulf Stream wells up out of the tropics to carry its warmth far along the east coast of North America across the Atlantic to make the British Isles and Scandinavia habitable. Imagine the rearrangement of world commerce that would result almost overnight from some new Pacific current, springing out of the south to bathe the vast coast of Siberia in a similar balm. Then there is the familiar semi-legendary, semi-actual vortex of the Atlantic: the Sargasso Sea with its acres of undulating weed and its tiny inhabitants, created and perpetuated by the blood stream of the great Atlantic currents, revolving majestically around it and confining it. I like to think, too, of the less-known Arctic currents: of wreckage of old Northwest Passage-seeking vessels turning up years later on the other side of Greenland; of Fridtjof Nansen's faith that the Arctic drift would carry his *Fram* over the top of the world while frozen solid in the ice. The whole subject is of limitless interest, especially to one who has sailed small craft over the oceans, for he who does this has a much closer and more intimate association with the great ocean currents than one can ever achieve in larger ships. When there is no wind we become an integral part of the current, partaking of its motion willingly or not, meeting its inhabitants, learning its peculiarities.

On my first voyage I had met the mighty Humboldt Current, the diametrical opposite of the Gulf Stream, pouring its cold waters from the Antarctic up along the coast of South America to the equator itself, and beyond; carrying with it to the equator offshoots of antarctic life, the sea lion and the little comic penguin; making two thousand miles of coast an endless rainless desert; creating for me the lure that was to draw us off at a tangent from our actual destination which was the Galapagos. I could not meet this cold ocean river again and not sail down it for at least a little way, following at the same time the sea trail of the old Spanish galleons and their enemies the buccaneers.

So when we finally left Panama it was with an unknown destination, depending upon the weather we might meet and the strength of the Humboldt. It was an uncertain thing for a small sailing craft to encounter the current and probable prevailing contrary winds. We would try to make Peru and the bird islands, but we were resigned to give up the idea if things went against us. In that case we would get as far south as we could, then swing west along the equator to the Galapagos if the southerly wind got too much for us. Actually, I had little hope that we would be so fortunate as to make Peru. Sometimes I even wondered if we ought to continue our seemingly ill-fated little expedition at all. Our succession of unfortunate adventures had delayed us half a year. Premature hurricanes in the Bahamas. Revolution in Cuba. Wrecked in the Central American jungle . . . So far everything had been against us. It was obvious that we sailed under a star that boded no good. But if we were always to think too carefully and be turned aside by a little bad luck we should get nowhere. And besides, there was the *Svaap*, rebuilt and ready to go, with her new and unique rig at last in its final perfected form, all thirty-two feet of her smooth and glistening. Out there, beyond Perico, lay the Pacific, vast and alluring for ever. . . .

We sailed from Balboa on January 23rd, 1934. For a few days we loitered in the Pearl Islands, getting into sea trim and stocking up with native produce for our voyage. We were five aboard now: Florence, Dan, myself, Sooky the honey bear, and Gaynose Wetmore the coati mundi, named for his long flexible inquisitive nose and for his jungle manners. Gaynose, whenever we caught a shimmering five-foot dolphin on our white feather jig, nearly turned

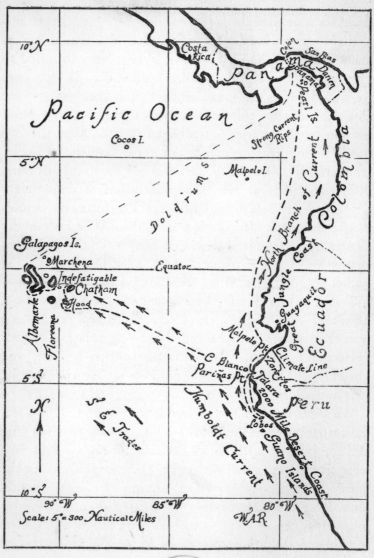

10°N

Costa Rica

Colón
San Blas
Darien

Panama

Panama

Pearl Is.

Pacific Ocean

Cocos I.

Strong Current
Rips

5°N

Malpelo I.

Doldrums

North Branch of Current

Colombia

Galapagos Is.

Marchena

Indefatigable

Chatham

Equator

Jungle Coast

Guayaquil

Ecuador

Albemarle

Floreana

Hood

Malpelo Pt.

Great

Climate Line

C. Blanco

Parinas Pt.

Tumbes

Talara

2000

Mile Desert Coast

Peru

5°S

N

Trades

Humboldt Current

Lobos

Guano Islands

10°S

90°W

85°W

80°W

Scale: 5° = 300 Nautical Miles

W.A.R.

inside out with excitement. Tied up, he excitedly tore at ropes, canvas, anything he could reach, until finally he got the whole tail end of the fish — a section as big as a dozen of himself. Then for two hours he would go at it ferociously with tooth and nail, eating until we feared he would burst.

On February 1st the palms of San José, southernmost of the Pearl Islands, blended into the dusk of evening astern. We were at sea — on the road of the Plate galleons. A firm, cool breeze caressed our sails and we slipped swiftly along bound for Peru.

The auspicious start, with its steady fair wind, gave us confidence that the new voyage held some recompense for what we had endured so far. And it was so. For a thousand miles we sailed, with fresh fair winds and a laughing sea. My faith in the Pacific was stronger than ever. We had turned the corner at last. Again the South Sea lay before us in all its enchanting entirety. The *Svaap* had the feel of other Pacific voyages now — that leaping rhythmic roll and rush of water along her hull. She was at home once more, as was I. We only endure the other oceans because we must, *Svaap* and I; the Pacific we love. ... The moon rose over the distant Cordilleras de los Andes. The sea was like stippled patent leather. The Southern Cross was our guide. We were steering due south.

Other days and nights ... We forged on through churning current rips that danced the *Svaap* about jerkily and sent odd pyramidal waves toppling over on her decks.

Once a distant roar threatened, ominously, followed by two great breakers that tossed our stern high in the air. In twenty-four hours we sailed a distance that had taken five days the last time I was there. The night wind was fair and strong, the morning breeze light and variable. Over the side on the end of a rope, each one of us in turn, to tow wildly along with the tumbling wake pulling cool at our bodies. Or in smoother weather to open our eyes under water and gaze beneath the boat into sapphire depths, and watch our little parasite fishes rush back from their shady home under the counter to see what curious creature was there, and scurry back to the security of their haven.

One hundred and twenty-five miles a day. A hundred and thirty. A hundred and forty . . . A school of sperm whales passed close, jumping mightily from the sea. One night one rose alongside to spout. The shower of it fell on Florence at the wheel, frightening her half to death. I held my breath for days — wondering when our fair wind would end. It was inconceivable it could have lasted so long. At night at the wheel I watched the constellations slip past overhead, choosing from time to time a new star by which to steer.

These were some of the most beautiful nights of my life — with phosphorescence that was dazzling. Great fish would blaze past, sweeping in reckless curves round and under our hull. The nights were already cooler, but without the penetrating chill they would have as we got deeper into the Humboldt Current. The tiny yellow point of light from the binnacle would hold my eye from time to time as I checked the star course I was holding. The dark moon shadows swept back and forth across the spinnakers, full and firm like the breasts of some goddess of the sea, dancing on a moonbeam, and my ship on dream waves. The rhythmic roll and surge and the tiny point of light before my eyes would become hypnotic. I would fall asleep in spite of all I could do. My head would drop. I would wake with a jerk, reach over for a handful of sea-water to throw on my face. Then again and again it would come and I would awake from a sharp blow on the forehead as my head hit the wheel in falling . . . until the first faint colours came in the east.

The coasts of Panama, Colombia, and Ecuador slid past, out of sight to the east of us. We kept fifty or sixty miles offshore, on the outer edge of the current, but we felt its growing strength in the increasing areas of eddies and rips. Then the equator, and an inconceivable sunset over a rose-coloured ocean. We were edging in toward the coast now, to avoid the more powerful arm of the Humboldt which is diverted to the west by Pariñas Point. This was the current that swung off to the north-west to flow through the Galapagos themselves. Still the northerly held and we sailed south — a thousand miles — into a long powerful swell straight out of the south: the advance guard of the south-east trade that we expected to break upon us at any time. For days, with the superstition of sailors, we avoided the subject of the fair wind, or how long it would last. Each noon when I would mark our day's run on the chart we three would glance surreptitiously at the steadily diminishing distance to Peru, at our steadily pulling twin spinnakers, but not a word would be said . . . so afraid were we that the spell would break that we hardly dared to breathe.

It was on the night of February 5th at ten o'clock that we sailed across the equator into the Southern Hemisphere, destination still uncertain but the prospect of making Peru getting brighter by the hour. And the next night we were abeam Santa Elena Point, the northerly approach to the Gulf of Guayaquil. We were still fifteen or twenty miles off and had not sighted land. And there, at last, the wind died. The ocean fell calm and glassy. Peru was almost in sight. It was time for the engine. In thirty-six hours we would be in Talara, the important northern port of Peru. From there it was only one hundred and thirty miles to the nearest of the Lobos Islands, the great bird rookeries that had become our present goal.

For once our engine failed us. The ignition went out, completely. Nothing I did would make it go. The next day there was a breeze, from the south at last, light and fickle at first but gaining in strength as it grew in confidence. We knew we had seen the last of our fair winds. And so we settled down to a weary beat across the wide gulf, on the other side of which lay Peru. To avoid the strength of the current and gain by any possible back eddies, we stayed within the protection of the gulf, working our way to the south. Our beautiful big main tris'l in its weird streamlined spar settled down to work and drew us steadily along, pointing much closer to the wind than we had ever done with our old rig. Closehauled like this she held as good a course by herself as if someone was at the wheel, so we let her go along alone, and the one on watch would read, or sew, free from the importunity of the wheel. But there was always someone on deck, for it does not do to grow lax. There are always squalls, or careless steamers to bring quick disaster to the unwary. When the haze of early morning lifted on February 8th we saw the mountains of Peru looming up ahead — the southern coast of the Gulf of Guayaquil.

We had long known that our most difficult job would be to pass Cape Blanco, the southern horn of the Gulf. There we would meet for the first time the full strength of the current and persistent head winds. Without the engine it might take us days to make Talara, just south of the Cape. We had to stop here to arrange with authorities at Lima for our permit for the Guano Islands. With plenty of time we would have done it under sail alone, but we had lost too much time already.

On my chart, dead ahead of us as we approached the Peruvian coast, was the name Zorritos which meant nothing to us. Our Sailing Directions described it as an oil town consisting of a number of oil derricks, tanks, and houses, and a population of about eight hundred, mostly employed by the petroleum company. This was evidently the beginning of the rich Peruvian oilfield region. Perhaps here we could get the engine repaired.

All day we crept closer to the coast, making slow

progress. Just before sunset we could make out the petroleum tanks and oil wells of Zorritos. Sunset that night was an extravagant spectacle beyond description, the loveliest by far that any of us had ever seen. Sunsets in Peru are something to live for. The low barren Arabian-like hills of the coast are capable of colour reflection such as one seldom sees. The temperature contrasts caused by the cold Humboldt waters create atmospheric conditions which almost guarantee sunsets and sunrises unequalled elsewhere. A thick haze settled over the land, and night closed down on us, as cold as a late autumn night at home. We lay off the coast and shivered.

Morning was unusually clear. Before us lay the panorama of one of Nature's great pranks. To the east lay Malpelo Point. Here ended the limitless jungle coast that stretched to the north along the shores of South America, and on and on the length of Central America: a practically unbroken jungle coast of dank mangrove swamps and savannahs, from Malpelo Point over there — low and green against the mist-shrouded hills — all the way to North America. It was the edge of one of the greatest jungles of the world that we gazed upon. But marvellous to behold: it ended there with a sharp finality that was hard to believe. To the south of the point was no more green. It was as though the Supreme Power had made a mark across the land, and said to the jungle: 'Beyond here you shall not pass!'

The same land, the same hills, rolled on to the south. The same Gulf bathed the shores. But the jungle and all vegetation ended, giving way to an arid desert, a rainless coastal belt thirty miles wide that stretched on into the south for nearly two thousand miles to the forests of southern Chile. Off this coast the Humboldt Current reigned supreme. The Humboldt Current — beginning and end of all interest in this coast. The Humboldt Current — cause of the impoverishment of the west coast of the continent and one of the greatest sources of natural riches anywhere, responsible for untold lives of cruel slavery and ten thousand hopeless deaths, for fortunes that ran to millions, for the degradation and remaking of a nation, and for one of the greatest field laboratories of science in the world.

CHAPTER XIV

EQUATORIAL ANTARCTICA

ALL visitors to the Peruvian coast are impressed by three outstanding features: the everlasting parched desert plains and mountains, the indescribable abundance of life in the sea, and the equally amazing bird life. Few have the opportunity to observe these things as intimately as we did on *Svaap*, or to study the strange sequence of life and natural forces that fit together like the pieces of a puzzle. The scientist can find a lifetime of work in the Humboldt, and a lifetime of interest. But one does not have to be a scientist to find the intricate workings of Nature engrossing. I am eager to go back there some day, and I am certainly not a scientist. The Humboldt gets in your blood, and well it might — for it is the most exciting of all the great ocean currents.

The Humboldt comes direct from the Antarctic and wells up against the continental shelf of South America way down south of latitude 40 south, and urged by the prevailing southerly winds of the coast follows the trend of the land northward in a great belt a hundred to a hundred and fifty miles wide, until after two thousand miles it reaches the westernmost extremity of the continent, Pariñas Point. Here the main body of the current turns off to the north-west through equatorial waters to the Galapagos, and loses itself in the vastness beyond. A lesser branch continues northward from Pariñas, affecting slightly the waters off the coast of Ecuador and Colombia. All through the main body of the current it retains amazing antarctic qualities, due of course to its cold waters. That great, but not very famous early observer, Alexander von Humboldt, whose name has been given to the current, first noticed the thick invisible plant life in the stream, and the hordes of smaller fishes which lived upon it, and the myriads of larger fishes and seabirds which preyed on the small fry, and connected this all with the low temperature of the waters off the coast. The prodigal chain of life in the Humboldt finds its ultimate source in the astonishing profusion of microscopic marine plants or diatoms. These tiny organisms are the fundamental food supply of all the creatures of the sea, and at second hand of the birds of the air above it. We, on the *Svaap*, often sailed through vast soupy areas actually coloured red from the masses of this microscopic life.[1]

Briefly the whole prolific life of the Humboldt Current

[1] I was especially interested in these beautiful, ever-varied snowflake forms of microscopic life, for I had on the voyage around the world collected many specimens from distant seas for my friend Dr. Albert Mann of the Carnegie Institution at Washington. Dr. Mann devoted his life to the study of diatoms

is based on the cold up-welling polar waters which bring to the surface, and thus to the diatoms, an endless source of food in the form of decomposed material from the bottom, rich nitrates which go through a marvellous cycle and end up eventually as the richest fertilizer, to be dug in the form of guano from the Peruvian islands, and shipped to the ends of the earth. The endless supply of this decomposed matter is responsible for a whole ocean river full of algae or diatoms. The diatoms are present almost everywhere in the surface regions of the seas, but here in such ideal conditions they are constantly present in vast excess.

Thus the chain of life: The Humboldt provides the basic elements of nourishment for living things in the form of the chemical results of decomposed matter. Nature provides the microscopic plants like the diatoms, capable of absorbing this material and preparing it for consumption by higher life. The smaller fish and crustaceans then come along and browse on the plentiful nourishing diatoms and grow fat. And the chain is well under way. The small fish multiply in unbelievable numbers and cover the surface waters of the current with their vast seething schools, pursued relentlessly by larger fish and sea lions. And thus the stage is set for the enormous flocks of sea birds, the most spectacular emblem of the waters of the Peruvian coast. They hover in clouds over the Hum-

and their increasing importance, not only in the field of pure science, but in connection with the food supply of the world, as the basic food of all fish life. On this Galapagos voyage, too, we were collecting diatoms, hoping to find again some new and beautiful forms.

boldt by day, and blacken the coastal islands' by night. They pursue the constantly migrating hordes of fish up and down the coast, but remain always within the confines of the current, growing to maturity, mating, raising their young, and finally dying here: the birds of the Humboldt Current. The sea birds gather and breed in fantastic numbers on the island rookeries, where they deposit their excrement which hardens and becomes guano. Man comes along after a while and digs up the vast accumulation, rich in nitrates, and ships it to his agricultural regions where it is used as fertilizer to raise abundant crops to nourish man. The larger fish in a more direct way go to nourish man, after having themselves consumed the small fish and thus the original chemical substances. Thus the fundamental chemicals in the sea, via the microscopic plant of algae and diatoms, go to nourish man in the end or perhaps not in the end, for I suppose some at least, of the same elements, find their way back into the sea eventually and there is neither ending nor beginning, but a continuous cycle.

Suppose you went south to the Bahamas for your vacation, and saw polar bears lumbering over the white sandy cays, or killing with their lightning paws the colourful fishes of the coral lagoons. Or suppose I wrote in this book that I was capsized in the Gulf of Panama by a herd of walrus. Yet it is no more fantastic to find albatross rookeries in the Galapagos in sight of the equator itself, or penguins, or sea lions, both of which are also found there and in the islands of Peru — in fact all along the

Humboldt Current. This unbelievable range for creatures of the antarctic is due to the cold waters of the Humboldt. The surrounding sea is the luscious warm Pacific, whose waters in these latitudes average perhaps 80° Fahrenheit. You can loll all day in the Pacific of these latitudes and feel no chill. And the mainland coast is also tropical. But in between runs this great ocean river, a hundred miles more in width — 20 degrees colder than the warm waters it thrusts aside. Dive into the water here and you soon come back aboard. And so, along this long ocean highway, creatures of the far south have found their way to the equator. Through countless generations they have adapted themselves to their new surroundings and have prospered. But they are still creatures of the far south to me — creatures of a land of snow and ice and glaciers, and as such they enriched those days and nights for me as we lay in equatorial waters, which became my equatorial antarctica.

We have not yet accounted for the two-thousand-mile coastal desert, for which the Humboldt is also blamed. Peru lies in the latitudes of the south-east trades, but before they reach the Peruvian coast they must past over the continent of South America. Coming across, they lose their moisture as rainfall on the eastern side of the Andes, the world's mightiest watershed. When they descend the Pacific slopes of the great range they are dry, becoming dryer still as they descend to coastal levels and the corresponding increase in atmospheric pressure raises their temperature. Thus the coastal region of Peru can expect no rainfall from this direction. Ordinarily, the daily sea breeze, the *virazon* of the coast, would bring in and deposit moisture on the land. But here the Humboldt gets in its work. For as the virazon slants up the coast, over the cold waters of the current, it becomes cold. Then when it finally strikes the coast the heat of the land immediately raises its temperature and thus its capacity for moisture. The sea wind sweeps over the hot land, and its moisture is not condensed until it reaches the coastal mountain tops, where it forms an almost permanent high fog bank — but even then no real rain. At night this strange fog bank settles down towards the sea, but never, or almost never, condenses into rain. Thus the great stretch of coast is barred for ever from becoming the verdant green land one would expect to find in these latitudes — fated to remain an eternal desert — until some sweeping climatic change occurs.

CHAPTER XV

THE INCA COAST

FOUR hundred years ago the same breeze, that now filled our sails and drew us along toward Zorritos, whipped the sails of another little vessel as she rounded to and let go her anchor off Tumbez, just beyond the point. For there, in 1527, Pizarro arrived in Peru with a clanking of armour, and the tiny seed was planted that was to grow into the ruthless conquest and merciless destruction of the Inca civilization. On the tedious way south most of the expedition had baulked and returned to Panama leaving Pizarro with fifteen men. With this ridiculous gaunt, half-starved spectre of an army Pizarro set out to discover and begin the conquest of Peru! The fantastic courage and initiative of these Spanish conquistadores is unbelievable. Setting out to conquer a continent with a dozen and two or three men! It has a grand romantic sound, but the story of Pizarro and his conquest is only to be futilely deplored as one of the bloodiest smears on the pages of civilization. Pizarro found an inconceivably rich and contented empire, more civilized (had he only known it!) than the entire known world of that time; more civilized — if the word has any meaning at all — than most of the world of to-day, with its war, revolution, poverty, and hate. Here was an empire welded together by the Incas, who deserve to go down in history as among the greatest political and social leaders of all time. For the Inca empire was composed of many tribes and individual languages, various older local civilizations, reaching from Ecuador far down into what is now Chile. Which speaks for itself of the strength and wisdom of the governmental system that could weld it together and hold it as a unified empire. It was a very complete social organization, a sort of monarchical socialism that radiated from the Inca down through officials of descending importance to reach all nooks and corners of the empire. The society was highly organized under the strong but benevolent government. Every citizen had a definite part to play, all for the good of the empire. The modern experiments of government along these lines could learn many a lesson from the Incas, for here was a social structure that worked, without unemployment or poverty, racial or labour wars. Life was completely organized. The people worked hard and the wealth poured into the hands of the Inca rulers and the priests, but this wealth was stored up and used when necessary for the good of the people.

They had built great highways. The main road, 1500 miles long, was one of Man's greatest engineering feats before the Machine Age, for its dizzy spans across gorges and valleys—masonry and suspension bridges unsurpassed to-day in design and execution. A rapid communication system bound the long empire together. The art and culture, the textiles and crafts, have rarely been equalled. The agricultural system was highly developed, including expert use of fertilizers and irrigation.

All this was to be destroyed in a few short years for the plunder and temporary enrichment of a few Spaniards, for although this advanced nation received Pizarro with civility and hospitality, it was raped, tortured and put to the sword, that the Spaniards might carry off the treasure of the land. A civilization was stripped of all it had developed through centuries of evolving art. Cities and temples were destroyed, more for the sport of it than anything else.

The extermination of the North American Indian is nothing in comparison, for this was but a restless primitive conglomeration of warring tribes of no great culture, and the only loss was human life and the heritage of a country — things of little value, it seems, in the world of progress. But the destruction of the Inca civilization is as though some small regiment of Europeans to-day were to sail to Bali, armed with avarice and modern implements of war, and torture, rape, and slay the peace-loving inhabitants, razing their temples and kampongs, in order to sail off with the gold and silver and jewels of the island.

In 1532 Pizarro delivered his great coup, capturing the great Inca Atahuallpa by treachery, slaughtering (as a sample of the really serious killing that was yet to come) two thousand of his unarmed followers, having lured them to a friendly meeting to exchange greetings and gifts. Atahuallpa, imprisoned, reached overhead and drew a line on the wall. For ransom he would fill the room to that mark with gold. His word was good. The treasure collected as a result is said to have reached a value of three million pounds.

Pizarro, it seems, was also imbued with the missionary spirit — that peculiar zeal which leads men to force their religion on other unwilling races. Atahuallpa was faced with the choice of accepting Christianity or being burned to death. He complied, as any sensible man would, and professed Christianity. So Pizarro relented and merely had him strangled to death with a bowstring. It is somehow suggestive of methods I have seen used by twentieth-century Christian missionaries to obtain converts among primitive peoples. The threat they use is of everlasting torture in a ghastly hell and other horrible forms of revenge that no kindly God would suffer to exist. It is usually efficacious among the credulous primitives whose belief in the supernatural makes them ready victims to the more highly perfected miracles and hells that the missionary has to offer. Modern missionaries fortunately have not the homicidal tendencies of the sixteenth-century ones, but whether they realize it or not the result of their work in many parts of the world with which I am familiar would have made Pizarro envious. Suppression of *joie de vivre* and age-old customs, imposition of unsuitable clothing and housing, deprivation of proper nourishment by missionary sects that consider diet part of religion (Christian workers fanatically setting the stage for tuberculosis) . . . these have resulted in greater mortality than Pizarro in Peru and Cortés in Mexico together accomplished.

It is rather amazing that in all that wealth-seeking empire of old Spain there was no one in a position of leadership with vision enough, when a God-given opportunity like this presented itself, to protect the goose that laid the golden eggs. Peru, ready to accept the white Gods as rulers, was presented to the Spaniards on a golden platter: a complete, unified colony producing wealth beyond even their wildest dreams. And they threw it all away for a few years of wild orgy.

One could hardly expect them to waste thought on such ephemeral subjects as the loss of a priceless art, or of the destruction of an advanced social and political system, or even of a unique and highly cultured civilization . . . but it is remarkable that they overlooked the far greater increase in wealth and power that would have come to them through colonizing these new races benevolently, developing their vast resources intelligently, enriching themselves and their nation for ever, instead of a mad insane orgy . . . and oblivion.

When Pizarro landed on this coast he found rich Inca palaces and temples. Four hundred years later we landed precariously at Zorritos in a difficult swell and found bristling oil wells, modern erections to a modern god. We landed somewhat in trepidation, with a disabled motor that urgently needed repair, and with no papers for Zorritos, for this was not a port of entry. From plentiful experience in other Latin-American countries we rather expected to be exploited for port charges, fines for irregular entry, overcharged for the repair job we needed. Actually we paid port charges of $5·00 — something to do with our entry without proper procedure. But the port captain was very decent about it, cutting the legal fee as stated in the books, by one-half. He told us the *Svaap* was the first yacht that had ever come to Zorritos. And he took us to lunch in the little wooden building that served as hotel. The Peruvian oil company that was the *raison d'être* of Zorritos, took their mechanic from his work so that by late afternoon the engine was running again. And they would take no money for the work. 'It is our pleasure, Señor!' And I remembered that I had read somewhere that the Peruvian was the gentleman of South America.

Zorritos is the northernmost of the Peruvian oil fields. It is a typical frontier town with its row of frame buildings along its only street. On all sides, between buildings, alongside the road, up on the hill, sprout the tall black oil derricks. The wells are pumped in the old-fashioned way — a central power plant linked to a string of wells by a long wire cable in turn connected to the various wells by levers.

The wire cable, more than an inch in diameter, moves back and forth slowly but methodically, pumping the wells. The most extraordinary thing about Zorritos is the fact that several of the wells are out in the sea, the derricks looking like a cluster of lighthouses. There was the same old familiar feel underfoot, and the unforgettable smell, of desert towns in Arabia or Egypt. That peculiar quality in the dust smell that one never forgets. The same withering dusty heat too — even the same topography. I had known that Peru would be like this, but it was strange, even so, to find the desert atmosphere that belongs somehow only to parts of the old world.

When night closed down we were well on the way to Cape Blanco under sail and power, anxious to have our bout with the Cape. Then the night fog closed about us, the first fog since we had left home. The tropics are usually fog-free, but now we were entering at last the real province of the Humboldt, and things were topsy-turvy. We stopped the motor and crept along the coast under sail with a gentle night wind. The distant rumble of surf told us when we came too close. We shivered in unaccustomed cold.

Dawn found us only a few miles from Cape Blanco, fighting the full force of the Humboldt Current. The early morning calm was followed by a fresh sea breeze from the south-west. Under full sail and power we plunged into our task, to pass what Dampier called the 'worst Cape in all the South-Seas to double'.

It is counted the worst Cape in all the South-Seas to double, passing to the Southward; for in all other places Ships may stand off to Sea 20 or 30 Leagues off, if they cannot get anything under the Shoar; but here they dare not do it: for, by relation of the Spaniards, they find a current setting NW which will carry a Ship off more in two Hours, than they can run in again in five. Besides, setting to the Northward they lose ground: therefore they always beat up in under the Shoar, which ofttimes they find very difficult, because the Wind commonly blows very strongly at SSW or S by W without altering; for here are never any Land-Winds.

If I were to rename Cape Blanco I should call it the Cape of the Sharks. They were not large sharks, only six or eight feet long, but they were there in droves. They escorted us and followed us, and aired their fins on all sides. We fell in with a fleet of picturesque pirates — native fishermen whose sails looked like Arab dhows from a short distance, adding to the illusion that we were back in the Red Sea again. Our confidence grew as we exchanged raucous greetings with the fishermen. If they could fish these waters under sail alone the Cape could not be so bad . . . and we were gaining steadily.

Like so many of the things which you have dreaded for long, the actuality holds nothing to fear and your troubles are much more likely to arise at some altogether unexpected time. So with Cape Blanco, which we had been dreading for so long. The forest of oil derricks lining the cliffs of the Cape slid abeam. The wind came in stronger and we bucked it and the current in short tacks, gaining slowly. The steep chop running over the long swells raced our propeller so that we had to stop the engine and continue under sail alone. By and by we could make out Talara through the glasses, almost invisible against the brown cliffs. Like a forest of denuded trees stood the oil derricks, a vast array stretching for miles inland, and south toward a rocky promontory which jutted out into the Pacific: Pariñas Point, the westernmost extremity of the continent.

When the afternoon breeze blew its strongest and the fishing boats from Talara came winging in off the sea, we came about a last time and sailed full speed for the face of the amber-coloured cliffs, racing the fishermen. The entrance was quite invisible. Then when we were close enough to see the rocks and buoys, a large steamer emerged from the heart of the cliff, heading north. We rounded the point into Talara Bay, taking off sail as we entered. Then to start the engine. Again it failed. We were in a bad spot. A narrow unfamiliar channel, a strong wind heading us. Up sail again, quickly. Short swift tacks in the channel, reading the directions in the Pilot Book as we go — for we have no chart of Talara. Full speed into the Pool — the protected inner basin of the harbour, coming smartly to anchor among a congested fleet of fishing craft, barges, and two tugboats.

We had officially reached Peru. Until this moment we had never been sure we could make it against the current. Luck had been with us. The engine had helped us only

for a very short stretch off Blanco. We could easily have
done it entirely under sail. The old sailors who had written so much of the difficulties of this stretch had had no
knowledge of modern close-sailing yachts. I think one
would have no real difficulty anywhere along this coast in
a well-found seaworthy boat able to go well to windward.
In any case the Islands of Peru were to be an actuality for
us. Galapagos could wait.

We stopped at Talara mainly to arrange for our permit
to go to the guano islands, which are strictly protected
against unauthorized visitors. The permit had to come
from Lima, the capital, but it was possible to arrange for
it by wire and mail from Talara. The red tape one must
go through, sailing about the world, even in so small a
craft as *Svaap*, is rather amazing. One who has had no
experience cruising in foreign waters would probably
expect that a small yacht sailing for adventure, without
commercial objectives, would be more or less free to come
and go as it pleased. Far from it. When I think of the
obstacles that we met at times I shudder for the commercial
vessels and what they go through. On this trip there was
more than the usual amount. Both the Galapagos and the
Lobos Islands required special permits and belonging
respectively to Ecuador and to Peru, it meant double negotiations. I am highly in favour of this particular red tape,
for it is an effort to prevent the reckless squandering of the
wild life of the islands which has always prevailed until
recently. Before leaving Panama we had to correspond

by wire with the Ecuadorean authorities at Quito. Eventually they authorized the Ecuadorean consul in Panama to issue our papers for the Galapagos, and for coastal Ecuadorean ports in case of need. This required much running about between the Ecuadorean consulate, the telegraph office, and the U.S. Legation, and took approximately two days of my time, and about the same for one of the men of the Legation. There was a possibility that unexpected circumstances might force us to call on the Colombian coast. So we visited the Colombian consul and arranged for this possibility. This took another half day, again assisted by the Legation. The Balboa authorities issued our Bill of Health, always required wherever you go. This had to be visaed. Then the clearance papers were issued. Another half day gone, so that altogether I spent approximately three whole days on the red tape of departure from Panama. We were not sure of reaching Peru, so we waited until reaching Talara before arranging for the Lobos Islands permit. There was communication by both telegraph and air mail here, and the embassy in Lima working for us — but we lost nine days waiting for this permit to arrive partly due to unusual delays in the mail. So that the actual time lost in red tape before we could sail for Lobos or Galapagos totalled twelve days of our time, plus a considerable amount lost by the legation in Panama and the embassy in Lima. Without the assistance of these two offices I hate to think what it would have been. The men in the diplomatic service were at all times more than eager to help us in every way, and we were greatly indebted to them. The port captain of Talara, Captain P. Mazure, a gentleman and a Peruvian, took it upon himself to waive all port charges for us when we left and upon our departure presented us with two bottles of Pisco, the Peruvian rum which is named after the town of the same name.

The delay in our permit for the Lobos Islands was not the fault of those who issued it. When the document finally came, accompanied by a friendly letter from Señor J. R. de la Puent of the guano authority, it gave us *carte blanche* in the islands, placing at our disposal every resource of the Compania Administradora de Guano. His letter of instructions to the agents, guardians and employees of the company on all guano islands was brief. It merely introduced us and went on:

> Please place yourself under their orders and give them all the facilities and materials they need and charge whatever expense they may incur to the account of the company.

That was all. But more complete hospitality and trust in strangers would be hard to find.

Most of the ports of Peru are open roadsteads with very unpleasant or even dangerous landing, exposed to the constant heavy swells and surf that are piled up by the powerful southerly winds. Talara is one of the rare exceptions, having the snug little cove called 'the Pool' into which vessels of moderate size come to load oil alongside the dock — receiving it through huge pipes at such a rate that you can actually see them settle into the water. In a few hours you can watch a huge tanker, empty, with scaly red bottom shamelessly exposed to public view, settle quietly and steadily down to her Plimsoll mark and depart. Vessels too large to enter the pool, moor to buoys offshore and receive their cargo of oil through a tremendous mile-long underwater pipe.

Talara is the headquarters for the International Petroleum Company, whose wells cover a large area in the vicinity and whose output makes Talara the most important port in Peru in value of shipping, exceeding even that of Callao, the port of the capital. Talara is really two towns; the rambling enclosed town of the Oil Company and its employees; and the hot dusty native settlement of a few thousand, lying just outside the gates of the company town. A few miles to the south, over a well-paved road and a tunnel through a hill, is Negritos, the other town of the company, located more centrally in the 'Field' as the oil-bearing region is called. All around are the parched desert plains and mountains. It is a frontier industry, in a frontier land, with the feel of its vast scope everywhere. It is rather thrilling to find out there in the desert miles of black skeleton towers bringing up from the bowels of the earth one of the most sought-after of all commodities. It was all a vast offering to the God of Power, a model of efficiency. The power plants of the wells thudding away ceaselessly. The great stills constantly operating. Rows of beautiful Diesel compressors echoing their staccato exhausts in the arid hills, the drills pounding away at new wells. Everywhere power, and more power, and cubic miles of potential power underground and in pipes and tanks. We stood by one of these new wells, just being capped — a deep one more than half a mile down. The next morning an unexpected gas pressure . . . a burst valve exploding like an H.E. shell . . a young superintendent standing by . . . and a young bride who had just come down on a recent boat went home again on the next a widow. For, in spite of all the efficiency, the God of Power demands a more special offering now and then.

The people of Talara, mostly American and Canadian, were very hospitable, as people in isolated spots are apt to be. But, as is also apt to occur in isolated places, social competiton had reached a fantastic stage. All salaries were paid by the company, which also provided the houses. These were placed on the level land near the port, and on the slopes of 'The Hill', and on 'The Hill' itself, where lived the manager, the higher officials, and a few other lucky families. The overwhelming ambition of everyone else in Talara was somehow, by hook or crook or impatient waiting, to acquire a house on 'The Hill'. As there were relatively few houses on this much-sought-after eminence there was a considerable amount of thwarted ambition, which took its outlet in other forms of social competition: in the quantity and value of personal possessions, and in competitive entertainment. The natural result was a group of tight social cliques, all friendly and hospitable toward the stranger, even vying to entertain him, but coldly courteous to one another. We were taken in generously, and very pleasantly entertained by all. But when, having accepted hospitality from someone in one faction, we dined the next time in another set, our first friends would regard us thereafter reproachfully and with less warmth. Similarly, when we became friendly with someone in a third group, the second would join the first in reproach. So that in a few days, trying to be equally courteous to all, we found ourselves in the awkward position of having offended all but the two or three who were above such small potato competition.

We learned a little of this part of Peru, of the little hidden valley oases, just like those in the great Asian deserts, where precious water gives life to a circle of green fertility, so unexpected in this land. We went back into the Pitch Mountains, the *Cerros de Brea*, where the Spaniards (and the buccaneers too, I suppose) used to go to get pitch to caulk their galleons. Here the precious oil that created Talara, Negritos, and the other north coastal towns, oozes to the surface by itself and can be had for the taking in small quantities. But those hot, thirsty miles over the desert, carrying it to the coast for the ships in the old days — they must have been hell.

The eastern shore of the Bay of Talara was littered with small fishing craft, anchored off or pulled up on the beach for repairs, among them some of the famous balsa boats that still navigate this coast. These are one of the most primitive forms of vessel still in use. I liked to walk along the shore and imagine myself several centuries back, when the balsas sailed all up and down this coast. The balsas to-day are simply smallish sailing rafts, with blunt up-curving bow, composed of a few big balsa logs lashed and pegged together. Since balsa wood has been adapted recently for various industrial purposes, due to its amazing lightness, we are all familiar with its cork-like quality, but it was still something of a shock when for the first time I saw a single man pick up a boat-raft composed of a half dozen telegraph poles, and carry it nonchalantly into the water. I later bought a balsa log considerably more than a foot in diameter and twenty-five feet long, with which I made an outrigger float for the canoe. Florence could lift this log alone.

Formerly the balsas were big capable sea-going vessels of two or three decks, rigged with mast and sails, which made long coastal voyages of a thousand miles and more. Dampier gives a good description of these boats, 'Bark-logs' as he calls them. They consisted, he writes, of a structure of three stories. A cellar half-submerged. The intermediate compartment for the men. And the top deck with its cargo of wine, oil, flour, sugar, etc. They could carry as much as sixty or seventy tons. The 'Bark-logs' of that time were used on trade to Panama in particular, where they disposed of the boat itself, as well as the cargo, for they were unable to beat back. The crew of three or four men would find other means of return. There are balsas to-day, some which are moved by oars stuck down astern and used as levers to push the craft forward, and others which have sails and go out at night with the land breeze and return in the afternoon with the sea wind. This is a safe enough occupation off this particular coast, with its dependable winds, but on the surface a seemingly hazardous adventure. Imagine sailing to sea, out of sight of land sometimes, on a little raft of a few logs.

The boats of the Inca coast are enchanting. The balsas, descended from one of man's earliest floating devices. The great sailing dugouts, like the *Volador* which had taken us from Garachiné to Panama, built of giant hardwood logs from the jungles of Ecuador. We saw some that were said to be over a century old, still in use. The more modern planked boats, reminiscent of the Red Sea or the Mediterranean, are themselves bright with character: broad, seaworthy, clumsily rigged, they are really the fisherman's home. He sails out in them into the Humboldt, 50 miles off and more, and stays out there self-sufficient for a week or two at times, cooking his simple fare over a charcoal brazier, utilizing the kindly ordered forces that Nature provides, grouped in little colourful fleets out there where the teeming bird flocks feed.

But of all the floating craft of the coast I like best the 'little horses', the caballitos of Peru, the little reed boats which the fisherman mounts like a hobby horse and guides out to the fishing grounds. Alexander Mann, a resident of Guayaquil who spent considerable time on this coast familiarizing himself with the caballito fishing, has some interesting notes on the art in his book, *Yachting on the Pacific*.

> They (the caballitos) are composed of bundles of coarse grass, tied together in the form of cigars

tapered to a point at both ends, the points being turned up to form bow and stern, the body of the buoy (for such it is) forming a deck across which the fisherman straddles, paddle in hand, his fish tied alongside his maritime steed, his provisions for the ten or twelve mile trip a handful of toasted maize and a flagon of water, his gear a stone as anchor, a handmade cord as cable, and hooks and lines . . . These unique craft are well adapted to withstand heavy swells, rising upon them as freely as a duck, and are carried inshore on the top of the surf and deposited at high-water line without damage or danger, the rider dismounting on dry land, shouldering his faithful steed, and carrying it to his hut . . . They instructed me in the philosophy of deep-sea line-fishing, which is to find a rocky bottom with seaweed growing upon it, to cast a well-baited hook with heavy sinker attached to the line, with a certainty of getting fish, the acme of the proceeding being the novel manner of distinguishing rock at from ten to sixty fathoms below the sea-level. The little steed is propelled to a spot supposed to be a likely one, the rider's bare legs in the water; it is stopped for observation, which is accomplished by placing the wooden paddle vertically in the water, its stock end up, to which is applied the ear; if very deep the teeth are placed in contact with the stock, a rippling sound being clearly noted over the rock, whilst a sandy or muddy bottom emits no noise. When the noise is heard these simple people say 'ya llora la peña', or 'the rock begins to cry', cast their stone anchor, and soon get plenty of fish.

Mann continues that he often checked the depths and

bottom claimed by the caballito fishermen and invariably found them to be correct. Thus the paddle of the caballito fisherman becomes an antecedent of the modern ship's Fathometer, both being merely a device to record sound waves echoed from the bottom of the sea. It is amusing to learn that one of the most expensive and recent inventions to aid the science of navigation, is merely a mechanical improvement on the fathometer the Peruvian fisherman astride his 'little horse' has used for centuries.

The officials of the International Petroleum Company were very kind. We were given all possible co-operation. We used the dance floor of the club-house as a sail loft, to cut a huge new spinnaker. A descendant of the Incas pedalled his sewing machine for hours while I fed the light material to him. Later I roped it myself, and when it was done it was a sail to be proud of. So the long wait was not so very long after all, but when our permit arrived one night at eleven o'clock on the company's lorry from Paita, the mail station, we hurried aboard and made ready to leave. At midnight, with a growing moon and a light night wind, we hove up the achor and sailed out into the Humboldt. Morning was too far away . . . we could wait no longer.

CHAPTER XVI

GUANO ISLANDS

THE night mist hung over the land but did not fall to the
sea. The moon shone through a golden archway in a
bank of clouds. Ashore, miles of twinkling lights along
the coast: and inland, the lights of the oil wells. The cold
of the Humboldt crept into our bones. Ahead, glowing
on the surface of the sea a lone steady light guided us south.
It was Pariñas, the western extremity of the continent. At
two in the morning we passed Pariñas. From its black
rocks came the bellowing of 'lobos', the sea lions that
would be with us from now on. The coast dropped away
to the eastward. Down there lay the Straits, and Cape

Horn. Some day perhaps . . . but not in *Svaap*, for *Svaap* is getting old—too old to have any ideas of that magnitude any more; but in a new *Svaap*, a little bigger, a little sturdier, we would perhaps see the rest of that coast that sloped away from Pariñas, a thin black strip in the moonlight . . . white mist hanging low.

Another day. Another night—forging steadily south into the current. This night the wind brought us the smell of the guano of Lobos, fifty miles away, which is my long-distance smelling record. The fog came down thick and heavy and it was colder than ever. The cabin thermometer registered sixty degrees. All night through the fog came splashings and breathings. As dawn came, and I could see in a little mist-bounded circle around me, the first life I saw was a whale who came very close, breathing, then threw up his barn door tail and dived under us. Other whales near by. The mist thinned a little—and there all around us on the uneasy oily waters lay a fleet of fishing boats, and a small steamer, uncertain of her position, steering uncertainly back and forth waiting for visibility. At ten-thirty the gentle morning breeze sprang up from the south and cleared the air. There was no land in sight, but we were in a new world.

The sea itself was a Neptune's broth of undulating red —alive with the microscopic plant life that enriches the Humboldt. Vast areas here and there were churned to a froth where tremendous schools of small fish (we later learned they were anchovies) were attacked from below by rushing hordes of larger fish and lobos, and from above by hysterical flocks of birds who threw themselves into the churning mess until the water was alive with the anchovies, larger fish, and birds. In between the areas of carnage the surface of the sea was coated with white acres of fresh droppings from other gorged flocks that hovered overhead. We could see no land but we knew the bird islands were close at hand. The birds about us were new to us. The great Humboldt pelican, so different from the little brown tropical pelican of Panama, Ecuador, and elsewhere. Streaming flocks of cormorants. Javelin-like piqueros. The gulls that followed our wake were Antarctic gulls, new to us. The flying fish were gone, and the rays and the tropical birds we knew so well: the magnificent fork-tailed man-o'-war, the lovely bo'sun bird . . . these had strayed down with us into the thinning waters of the Humboldt along the coast as far as Peru. But now we were in the real domain of the current and they were with us no longer.

We were fifty miles offshore, but dozens, almost hundreds of little Peruvian fishing boats with their Arabian dhow sails were about us — little open boats, not fit for heavy weather. A little water and food aboard — fifty miles offshore! But they have nothing to fear. Nature here is kind. The land breeze at night takes them out part way, the virazon carries them where they want to go in the fishing grounds, and will bring them home again. Never a strong offshore wind to bring danger. Never a storm to upset the plan of their lives. For all days are alike in the Humboldt . . . the gentle night wind, the morning calm, misty, with a dreamy mirage quality like the Arabian coast of the Red Sea, then the virazon — always from southerly quarters — starting unassuming enough but working up to considerable proportions in the afternoon, reefing strength at times, and then the peaceful calm of the evening. The fishing boats often stay out for days, working constantly to windward when they can, to balance the current, drifting to a sea anchor occasionally, when it is calm or when the virazon blows too strong. They often fish by night when the sea is calm — drawing their seines around the fiery phosphorescent areas of fish. And then when they are ready they lift their sails and slant away across the current back home again with holds full of drying fish. Theirs is a strange, calm, placid life, filled with a sureness unknown to most fishermen the world over. Like a cog partaking of the regularity of a well-oiled mechanism, they have fitted themselves into the scheme of things, perfectly in tune with their world.

At noon a faint brown smudge on the hazy horizon. Lobos de Tierra rose from the sea under a halo of birds, which was fitting. Beyond, over the horizon to the south, lay Lobos de Afuera. The day had a peculiar unreal dreamlike quality hard to describe, with a feeling of mirage all about so that you were not sure of what you saw. And the fleet of little operatic boats sailing in all directions, the foolish steamer at last sure of herself steering off to the north-west with a kind of 'I knew it all the time' air, the legions of small fish leaping out of the sea and the legions of birds plunging into the sea . . . even that streak of island on the horizon . . . it all seemed to be part of a strange throbbing dream, full of meaning but bewilderingly vague.

We came abreast the southern end of Lobos de Tierra at two o'clock, sailing fast into the customary afternoon wind. We had had a current of two knots against us all the way, setting strongly north-west. Rounding the southern rocks, sailing through ducks, pelicans, piqueros, sharks and sea lions, we fell off before the wind and coasted the eastern shore, following the bays as we went, picking up landmark after landmark. Larrañaza, a cosy little anchorage sometimes used by the fishing boats. White Rock, packed with birds on every available inch, and sea lions too. There was a beautiful narrow inshore passage here, deep and safe. We passed Black Stone with the swell breaking sullenly on it, and Juanchuquita Bay opened before us. Four tall spars appeared. Then a hull — a ship at anchor. Then we saw that it was a wreck, but in excellent preservation. It was in almost enough water, so that it rested on even keel. All over it, on spars, fittings, decks, hatches — the inescapable birds. The Pilot Book said that the government guardian lived in Vivero Bay on the north-west side. We were sailing entirely around the island first, just to survey our field of activity. There were buildings in Juanchuquita Bay, several of them, but we thought they must be abandoned guano works. Past the bay was another wreck, a ship in two halves a hundred yards or so apart, well up on the rocks. It too was black with birds. As we rounded to the northern coast the surge was sweeping violently upon Cape Cross, booming in its caverns. But the wind was strong and dependable and we sailed along only a boat's length from the jagged rocks, so close that we frightened our first little group of penguins from their afternoon siesta on the rocks. They walked gravely to the precipitous edge and dived in, reappearing a moment later near the *Svaap*, impertinent and curious. The other birds were too indifferent to budge, but sat in black and white masses on the rocks, watching us boredly. We passed close to the great offshore rock called Albatross Island, lacking at the time those great flyers, but well supplied with sea lions and guano birds. The tortured bellowings of the lobos filled the air with reverberations. These happy care-free animals are for some reason fated to go through life conversing with one another in the agonized wailings of souls in purgatory. There was a magnificent natural arch through which the sea broke in white glory — with a rainbow crown as the sun's rays slanted through the opening.

Finally we came to Vivero Bay, the supposed headquarters. We scouted its shores but found it to be a very bad anchorage, rough and uncomfortable, with no landing except through heavy breakers on a steep beach. Nor was there any sign of human habitation. So back around Cape Cross again to Juanchuquita Bay, obviously the place we wanted. We sounded our way in, for here the water was clouded with minute life. Then a boat put off from the skeleton pier. The guardian and his men read our permit and said they were ours to call upon. As we anchored the sky was filled with files of homeward-bound birds. Vast flocks of pelicans were settling on the island in masses. Long undulating columns of guanayes came in from the sea — endless rivers of birds — and performed graceful figures before landing. It was homing time. The island was undergoing a curious transformation. It had been blazing white in colour, almost blinding before. The bare guano-covered rocks caught and reflected the low rays of the sun, making it appear like an Arctic island of snow and ice. A strange glazing process that takes place on the surface of the guano, called 'guano glass', adds to this effect, giving a glacier-like appearance. Incidentally, the glare from this kind of guano is as hard on the eyes as Arctic glare, and I believe it could cause snow-blindness if not guarded against. The island had been semi-populated before — with black areas of the colonies here and there. But now, as the birds came home in clouds from all points of the compass, and flight after flight settled on the island, the black areas grew and spread, over-lapping in places, until the whole appearance of the island had changed. All except the steep glazed ridges, which still shone icy white in the last rays of the setting sun. The colonies became so crowded that there was standing room only; and yet more flights came in and squeezed somehow into the press. The island men departed, but we stayed aboard. It was enough for one day merely to sit on deck and watch the spectacle. Besides, it was nearly night. Near by, the old four-masted ship grew black — outlined against the sunset sky. The pungent ammoniacal smell of the guano thickened the air. It grew cold the moment the sun had gone. We went below into the comfort of the cabin and the more pleasing odour of cooking supper. To-morrow we would explore our first guano island.

Second only to the Humboldt Current in interest, guano becomes so self-evident that it is impossible to get away from it. It is a major topic of conversation all down the coast. You see it covering the islands. You smell it in the air when the islands are long out of sight. You probably learn for the first time exactly what it is and why it is important. To put it starkly, guano is the excrement of millions of sea birds, deposited on their island rookeries in such amazing quantities that some of the islands were built up to almost double their natural altitude. It is said that during the halcyon days of the guano trade some of the islands were cut down 100 feet and more in height before the workers came to bed rock. Imagine square miles of land built up 100 to 150 feet by the simple addition of bird droppings! And imagine the fish that went to make this. The birds responsible for such an astonishing situation are mainly boobies, cormorants, and pelicans. There is the great *alcatraz*, the Humboldt pelican, a gross bulky bird fifteen pounds and more in weight whose wings spread more than six feet. Floating on the water they look more like huge grotesque children's toys than birds of flesh and blood. The Humboldt cormorant, locally known as the *guanay*, is a smaller bird somewhat like a penguin, and in fact it resembles the little *pajaro niño* or 'child bird' so much that we were often deceived from a distance when we saw them standing on the rocks close to the sea. The outstanding feature of the guanayes is their beautiful flight, in endless undulating files — like a snake dance on the wing, extending into infinity. All the other birds fly in packed cloud formation, or in small groups, but the guanayes make one think of spring in the north and the wild geese migrating — but on a scale the wild geese never dreamed of, single columns often extending out of sight over both horizons. The other two great guano birds are boobies: the 'piquero' or 'lancer' of the Spanish, unrivalled anywhere in its spectacular diving: and the 'camanay', whose wide webbed feet are a strikingly violent blue. All of these four birds except the camanay are peculiar to the Humboldt. The camanay of the blue feet is found in many isles of the tropic seas.

Between them, these four birds are the producers of the invaluable Peruvian guano which is so high in nitrogen content that it is one of the richest fertilizers in the world. The desert climate of the islands keeps the guano deposits unspoiled, so that the Humboldt is not only reponsible for its production, but for its preservation as well. Not only the moderns, but the ancient people of the coast too, the Incas, appreciated the value of guano. The Incas developed a whole agricultural system based upon it, controlling its extraction and protecting the birds who produced it.

The guano islands, many of them only islets, extend all along the Peruvian coast, all more or less similar, utterly void of vegetation, white by day from their coating of guano, blackening in the evening as the vast flocks return for the night. The islands are rugged, sea-worn, with coastal caves and water-worn arches. Northernmost of the islands is Lobos, consisting of Lobos de Tierra or 'sea lions near shore' and Lobos de Afuera or 'sea lions offshore'. The other islands string along to the south, names famous in the middle of the last century when the great guano trade flourished and the squareriggers engaged in the trade were numbered by hundreds: Gauñape, Mazorca, Pescadores, Can Lorenzo, Chincha, Ballesta, San Gallam, and many more.

The guano rush was in its prime in the middle of the last century. For the few short decades it lasted it was a remarkable thing, romantic in spite of the unpleasant cargos and inhuman methods used. Scores of great squareriggers raced around the Horn, and around the world, with their holds full of the choking dead weight of guano, or lay in the harbours of a hundred ports while the crimps combed the waterfronts to snatch new crews for another voyage after the loathsome stuff. A side-line was the running of Chinese coolies, ostensibly recruited under contract, actually to slave hopelessly on the islands, digging with pick and shovel at the guano until the sun killed them or they died of exhaustion, or possibly committed suicide in despair as many did. The well-filled Chinese graveyards we found, surrrounded and covered with guano, emphasized the sordid history to us vividly.

The now deserted islands thus had a considerable population. When possible, the skippers warped their ships' sterns close under the cliffs and the stuff was poured into their capacious holds from above through huge canvas chutes. Otherwise it was lightered out. The cargos reached placid destinations on the Chesapeake, London . . . . wherever there was a demand for the rich fertilizer.

The Incas had taken guano from the bird islands for many hundreds of years. Confronted by the great desert coast, they developed an amazing agricultural science, throwing irrigation canals all over the coastward slopes of the hills, boring tunnels through awkward ridges, using the guano fertilizer to enrich the land. They rigidly protected the birds that gave them the guano and carefully controlled its extraction in order to conserve the supply.

In the 1840's — when the modern exploitation era began, civilization brought new methods to take the place of those of the ignorant savage. The birds were in the way, a nuisance, so they were killed and driven away. The islands were hacked and dug at frantically as men sought to get rich quick, the quicker the better. It is said 'that more than ten million tons were extracted between 1851 and 1872 from one small group of islands. A single island, it is said, was lowered more than a hundred feet by the removal of its thick crown of guano. The possibility of exhaustion of the deposits was not then contemplated, and no thought was given to conserving the birds'.[1]

The national finances of the country were run almost

[1] R. E. Coker, *National Geographic Magazine*, June, 1920.

entirely on guano. There was nothing to worry about. God had been kind. . . . Then finally Peru woke up and found herself without any guano. The islands had been scraped down to bed rock. The birds were gone, so the deposits were not being renewed. Now modern Peru has changed all that. There is the national guano administration, an organization of foresight and vision. The islands have been made perpetual bird preserves. The flocks have returned and increased so that they have almost reached the proportions of Inca days. The guano is increasing and is already providing a modest income for Peru. The islands are worked in rotation at intervals disturbing the birds as little as possible, and the birds are left entirely undisturbed the rest of the time.

The Peruvian islands had brought us far from our course. And after this long trip we visited only Lobos. I suppose it may be wondered why we went to all the trouble. It would be easy to assume a righteous air and say that we came in the interests of science. We did do a little scientific work, collecting microscopic marine life, and so on, but in the interests of honesty I will admit that we really came for the fun of it, which I suppose is the real reason we were going to the Galapagos.

It is one of those things that are so close to the heart that it is next to impossible to convey them clearly to others. Why did I sail around the world in the *Svaap*? Or up the Sambu? Or back to the Galapagos? Or plan to go to the Arctic? Frankly I couldn't answer clearly for I don't really know myself. It is a complex blend of urges: a love of the sea for one, that takes the curious form of wanting to meet it face to face on the most equal of terms, instead of from the one-sided vantage of a liner's deck. Perhaps it is an attempt to accomplish difficult things in such a way that I can flatter my ego by saying to myself: You have done this thing alone, with your own two hands. It is partly that I find more beauty in life away from the turmoil of the twentieth century existence, and partly a compelling interest in the primitive lands and people.

But fundamentally, I think, my life is an effort to live down as best I can the knowledge that I am two hundred years too late. Could I have chosen the time when I was to live, I would without a moment's hesitation have asked for the time when the great era of discovery by sea was just beginning; when men were starting to push back their walls of geographical ignorance . . . To have been the first, for instance, to sail around the tip of South America into the vast unknown Pacific, and look for the first time upon those lovely coral archipelagos and fantastic towering peaks beyond. The nearest one can come to all this is to sail in small ships with as few as possible, navigating yourself, becoming a little world of your own from which you can exclude the knowledge that great steamers and motor vessels have, as like as not, been over the very same course before you. And of course, with a very small ship like ours, we can go to a thousand places where larger ships can never go, and there sail almost if not quite virgin seas. With so little to destroy the illusion you can come nearest to achieving the seventeenth- or eighteenth-century feeling — the exquisite adventure of seas that are still vast and limitless, a horizon beyond which might lie anything, or nothing.

But this is all far from the subject. Now that we were in Lobos we were going to make photographic studies of the bird life. This meant work. The letter from Señor de la Puent was a great boon, for we needed help to carry the clumsy motion picture cameras over the hot dusty slopes. The next day was Sunday, which did not mean a day of rest for us, for it was our day to clean ship, even though it was our first day in port. So it was afternoon before we were ready to go ashore. A huge flag flew from the guardian's headquarters in our honour. Beneath it sat almost the entire population of the island, waiting. There was Gregorio Monsalve, the guardian. Gregorio had been twelve years in the guano service, but only one year on Lobos. Then there was Enrique Marquez, the kindly stuttering lighthouse keeper, whose twenty-four years in his lighthouse had left him still generous and eager to please. And there were two workmen, under Gregorio. Enrique Marquez had left his family at home by the lighthouse, about an hour and a half's walk from here. They completed the population. Gregorio and Enrique both took an acute interest in our work, and had we had no interest in the birds we should have been shamed into it by the enthusiasm of Gregorio. It was easy to see that he was an excellent guardian for his charges. There were nesting boobies raising their families at his very doorstep.

The Juanchuquita Bay region had been taken over by the pelicans. Gregorio set off almost at once to take us through the colony, explaining as he went, giving the Spanish names for all stages of growth, telling us everything he could think of about the birds. Our Spanish was less than sketchy, and he knew only Spanish, but he had a quick wit and was good at putting an idea across in spite of linguistic handicaps. I had been on island bird rookeries before, in Galapagos, in Mopelia, and elsewhere, but this was a new experience. As we progressed a solid wall of adult pelicans swept across the ground a few feet ahead of us, down slope, getting speed for their take off. They had a curious lumbering gait, accompanied by violent flapping of creaking wings which stirred up vast clouds of dust. They looked quite unable to get off the ground, like an early attempt at a flying machine, and often found it necessary to cast off ballast by vomiting up their latest meal. But once in the air they became stately, magnificent flyers. As we walked along there was always the solid wave taking off just ahead, the myriads overhead that shut out the sun, and behind, the earlier waves settling back to earth again, so we moved forward in a little open space which remained centred about our feet.

It was breeding time. The ground was covered with nests, little hollows in the guano with eggs or miserable naked leathery pelican chicks, sickly purple in colour, the most repulsive form of infant life I have ever seen. The gawky homely half-grown fledglings with faces a hundred years old massed together in groups a little apart, jostling and tumbling over each other in an awkward effort to retreat *en masse*, also ejecting fish in their excitement. Young and old, the pelicans are all the same: the clumsy, moronic member of the guano bird tribes. They did not even have sense enough to try to defend their homes, as did the other birds we visited later, or to keep from walking on their own eggs. They kept a peculiar dumb silence through their excitement, or a low muttering in the case of the excited fledglings.

We learned that first day that the birds themselves all stank abominably and that they were infested with lice and ticks. The ticks were not interested in us, but the lice got all over us and were a constant annoyance.

We cut across the island at the narrowest part and came to Vivero Bay, where gorgeous scarlet and purple crabs raced up and down the beach between tremendous breakers. When the guanay files came winging in from the sea we started home weary and dirty. I have never appreciated my evening plunge as much as I did at Lobos. Gregorio left us at the pier, to return to his headquarters. For him there was no escape from the guano dust.

We started out one day, just Florence and I, to circumnavigate the island on foot. Dan had gone off sketching. The island is five and a half miles long and

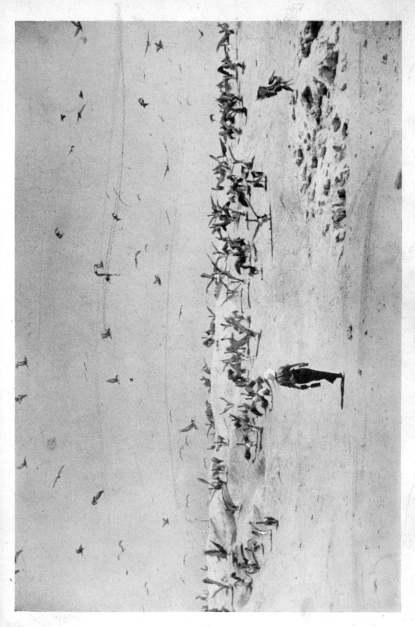

Young pelicans scatter from the nesting grounds at Mrs. Robinson's approach

less than half as wide, narrowing between Vivero and
Juanchuquita Bays to an isthmus that almost divides it
into two islands. It took us the whole day to get around
the northern half and back to the isthmus. Starting
toward the north along the east coast we walked through
two miles of pelican colonies. They infested the shores,
the old fallen-in piers, the wreck that was in two halves
. . . everywhere pelicans, until the rocky inhospitable
ridges of the Cape Cross region blocked them off. Here,
in surf-beaten little coves and gorges between undercut
cliffs, were hundreds of lobos, gigantic great bulls vastly
larger than those in Galapagos, and their harems of sleek
stream-lined cows. Here and there a little cluster of shy
penguins. We climbed a high pinnacle over Cape Cross
to eat our meagre lunch of chocolate, ship's biscuit, and
dried peaches. Gay little Tropidurus lizards darted after
our crumbs. On an adjoining pinnacle, a few feet off,
perched three black turkey buzzards, or vultures, called
gallinazo. By spreading their wings they would soar
motionless in the air currents, hovering within arm's
length of us, staring at us with baleful glassy eye. They
were without fear. We were to have a loathsome experience with them later. Straight down below us was a
family of the great lobos, hoisted out of the surf on to
abrupt shelving rocks. Once a stray bull came investi-
gating, and the lord and master lurched himself to the
edge and catapulted after the intruder with terrifying
bellows. The home must be protected at all costs, even
when you have twenty wives. A yellowish blur in the

distance was Peru, the mainland south of Aguja Point. In the strait between we could see lines of surf-foam streaming away to the northwest, clearly showing the direction and force of the current.

The west coast as far as Vivero Bay proved to be less populated than the east coast had been. There were a few pelican colonies and as we moved south increasing numbers of piqueros and guanayes. Again there were magnificent breakers in Vivero Bay. The backwash from the steep beach was so heavy that it made great white geysers when it met the new wave. It was getting too late to continue. We had been baked by the glaring reflected heat — the parts of a guano island sheltered from the southerly winds are exhaustingly hot — so we found a rocky pool, threw off our hot, flea-ridden clothes, and dived into the shockingly cold water. Then a short walk across the narrow isthmus and we were home.

We remained in Juanchuquita Bay until we had completed our work with the pelicans, Gregorio keeping our noses to the grindstone, carrying our camera equipment all over the place. Others have written in detail of the birds of Peru, so I will avoid that.

Every evening we sat on deck or on the beach, with its thick seaweed and great squid cast up by the tide, and watched the endless undulating files of guanayes streaming past our heads to their colonies on the southern part of the island. And so one day Enrique Marquez arrived from his lighthouse to pilot us round into a miniature cove on the south-west side of the island.

From there we could more easily work among the piqueros and guanayes. It was one of those standard, breathless pastel mornings of the Humboldt, misty and unreal. Over on the mainland side of the strait there was real fog. We retraced our trail of the first day, past White Rock and Nopo, along the placid eastern coast. A half-dozen long crescent beaches. A few offshore rocks. We sailed straight through one of those maelstroms of diving piqueros and a living thrashing sea of anchobetas, bonitos, and lobos — the most spectacular sight of the Humboldt. The piqueros, those greatest divers of all, hurtling down like flights of white arrows, a living rain aimed at the hapless anchobetas. Only motion pictures can describe a vibrating feathery sky vomiting whole clouds of piqueros into the sea, miraculously missing the thousands ahead of them popping to the surface after their dive, slanting away low over the water to gain altitude for another piercing descent. But even sound pictures could not record the cacophony of wild bird cries, the thrashing living waters, the electric excitement that crackles through the air. We sailed through billowing rafts of stuffed guanayes, resting until the process of digestion allowed them to resume. These were surface fishermen, not divers. The pelicans, too, would float on the surface, lift their great bodies out of the water, glide a few feet at a low angle, plunge into the school and float again, gobbling their fish. But the boobies, and the piqueros in particular, would dive fifty or seventy feet straight down like a flash, never missing.

As we approached the end of the island the flocks were going about their amazing business, long sinuous guanaye rivers stringing out to the north, boobies inexplicably going in the opposite direction, answering some mysterious call, files and flocks criss-crossing, over and under, interlacing, weaving a changing pattern in the sky. They were flying low, and the air throbbed with a million wingbeats. Our ears sung with a strange song of dynamos in a power house . . . until the anchovies broke the surface again some distance off, driven by the bonito schools and the roving sporting lobos who made a game of the business of life, rushing after the fish like torpedoes, leaping into the air one after the other, turning somersaults, circling the *Svaap*.

We rounded the south point of Lobos de Tierra and followed the broken, cliffy west coast a little, to Cherra Bay, where Enrique showed us the way into a nest of rocky coves, in one of which we anchored, quite landlocked, almost squeezed in by the jagged cliffs on three sides, and a tiny beach on the other. It was one of the most picturesque spots the *Svaap* has ever been in. I have never seen water more vividly coloured, sapphire and emerald, nor reflections so startling. If you paddled a hundred yards out you would never dream the cove was there, and as for an ocean-going ketch . . . there was nothing but jagged rocky cliffs. I could well understand why the buccaneers had chosen to lie in wait in Lobos, hidden from the world, with a look-out on the hill to watch for unsuspecting Spanish galleons, plying between Panama and Lima, then the centre of Spanish power in America. Incidentally, the story of the buccaneers as told by William Dampier in *A New Voyage Round the World* has very interesting material concerning this coast, and these islands, as well as the Galapagos.

On the little crescent of beach a half-dozen fishermen from the mainland had a temporary camp where they were making *bacalau*, rather like dried codfish. They were also salting down small sharks and rays, all of strangely uniform size. Above, on the top of the highest hill of the island, stood the lighthouse, three hundred feet above sea level, a fine modern light with a twenty-six-mile visibility if there is no fog, which I am afraid is seldom.

The guano islands are hardly noted for their beauty, but Caleta de Cherra was one of the most fantastically beautiful spots I have been in — a jumble of miniature opera scenery stuck around the amazing little blue cove. It was something like Capri, in miniature, more unexpected, more changing as the lights changed through the day. It was a wonderful place to climb and explore. Climbing over a ridge suddenly you would come upon a little hollow, with several couples of blue-footed boobies doing their grotesque mating dance — intent and serious — bowing, stepping, strutting, balancing, repeating — talking all the while, the male in his pleading whistle, the female in her blaring honk — both utterly oblivious of the fact that they were not alone in the world, of the fact that a wing-spread away from them on either side, other couples were going through the identical evolutions, equally oblivious. It was like a strange old European folk dance. The gestures made me think of the pantomime of Mohammedans, praying at the call of the *muezzin*.

The breeding season is more or less continuous. Near the courting birds would be other pairs, taking turns at guarding the eggs, still others being plagued by full grown chicks for more and more fish. The baby boobies are the prettiest bird children I have ever seen, just as the pelicans are the ugliest. They grow to adult size before losing their snow-white baby down, and are like an enormous powder puff. The boobies were also the bravest. When we came too close they stood their ground, spearing at us with their rapier-like beaks, the female trumpeting her anger in a loud hoarse voice. The male had quite a different voice, a queer whistling sound like a winter blizzard whistling in gusts through crevices.

In the tiny cove next to ours lived a family of penguins, shy, fat little creatures that spent their days swimming and diving, or standing with great dignity on the shore ledges to sun themselves. They were bigger than the little Galapagos penguin, but nowhere near as large as the Antarctic ones.

We were surprised to find that stuttering shy Enrique was the head of a little clan of eleven souls, living up there in shacks below the light, which was their whole existence. There were cats, dogs, and chickens. We remembered that the food and water for all had to come from the mainland. They were all kindly hospitable people, giving us what few delicacies they had, breaking our hearts to have to accept them, knowing what little they possessed. But they had the lighthouse at sunrise, and the whole sea-world round about their island in mid-morning when the first tentative breaths of the virazon begin to scatter the dreamy mists and pastels over the surrounding sea and the golden hills of Peru beyond. They had a lifetime of Humboldt sunsets. So on second thoughts perhaps Enrique knows what he is about — he had his twenty-four years up there.

As we stood on the little iron platform high up beside the great beacon — braced strong against the virazon — we could actually see the current sweeping past. Down below, unless you were sailor enough to discover the current by the difference in wave form, you might not realize its strength. But from this elevation on a small island we could actually see the great Humboldt river sweeping past to the north-west. From each end of the island it snatched a streamer of foam from the surf on the rocks, and drew it along with it on its course in a wavering ribbon that disappeared over the horizon. Farther out to sea, and also in the strait, were other parallel foam lines, perhaps from other islands down to the south, all undulating like so many endless sea-snakes — hurrying toward the equator. Up there by the light, you had the feeling of being on an island that was moving through the water into the south.

At night the moon silvered the island. It was impossible to believe that we were in the tropics. The glazing on the rocks reflected the light like ice. Surely we were afloat in the heart of an iceberg.

It was here that we were the sorry victims of the most horrible jest I have ever known. I have mentioned the gallinazo — the red-headed turkey vulture of these islands. It is a giant bird, utterly without fear as I have said. We were at lunch one day, aboard *Svaap*. Suddenly something happened I hope will never occur again, to us or to anyone else. Through the open hatch, and the companionway, came a sudden rain of putrid gelatinous fish skeletons, half-digested baby birds, sticky feathers, feet and skulls. All over Dan's spick and span galley, splashing into the stove and a pot full of something cooking. The companion steps dripped the awful stuff. It even rained through the cabin skylight on to the cabin table.

Seven great gallinazos perched on the spring-stay overhead, having recently gorged on fledgeling birds, and indirectly on the small fish the unfortunate birds had taken from their mother's crop at their last meal. There is an old joke which expresses relief that cows don't fly. I would rather be under a hundred cows than beneath one gallinazo! Any day! I shot the birds, methodically, once I had managed an exit from the terrible place. Bang — one bird. Bang — another. Bang — a third. . . . Absolutely disdainful of man, they sat there like ninepins while I dropped them one after the other. Some fell into the water, some on deck with a heavy thud. Even the bodies gave off a horrible stench. We had to improvise gas-masks to re-enter the cabin. We scraped and scoured and disinfected — but for days the *Svaap* smelled from the horrid bombardments. Thenceforth we never left a hatch or skylight open, and we always carried a gun to revenge ourselves on the whole race of gallinazos when opportunity came. They never came in sevens again, but usually when we returned there would be one or two, and the corresponding deck-washing job.

It was only a short march across the island from Cherra Bay to Nopo Bay where the biggest piquero colonies were. They were packed even closer, if anything, than the pelicans of Juanchiquita Bay. When they came in at the end of a day's fishing it seemed impossible that they could find a place to stand. We worked hard with the motion picture cameras and with the marvellous little Leica that does all my still photography.

Near by too were the guanay colonies, although they were not in such numbers as the other two species. They were brave too, almost as brave as the camanayes. They would stand their ground, feathers all on end, hissing at us and nodding menacingly. The pelicans and the piqueros would always retreat, abandoning everything to the stranger, which is rather odd, since all kinds are so closely related in lives and history.

Enrique had taken the place of Gregorio and was constantly in readiness to help in every way. I think Enrique's greatest pleasure was in showing us 'The

Tree'. This tree was near our cove. It was a very special kind of a tree, famous in its way, for Enrique told us that it was the only tree in the guano islands of Peru. It was a scraggy, misshapen, thorny little thing, three feet high. Enrique took such pride in the tree that I naturally assumed that he had planted it himself. Much to my surprise he said that it had always been there, as far back as the lore of the island went. Man puts great value in trees and plants when he hasn't got them. The people of the coast work for years to get a few green things to grow by their homes, carrying soil and water at great pains. It is hard to realize how much these things mean to us until we are deprived of them. I shall never forget my almost delirious joy when, after months in Arabia, we came to Suez with its wealth of foliage, grass, and flowers. And so with Enrique — that dwarfed shrivelled little tree, eking out a wasted existence where no other tree had ever grown, meant so much to him that it was pathetic.

When we bathed, Florence and I would take the canoe, soap, and the diatom dredge. Then in some little rocky cove with a few feet of sand at its head and rich waters surging in and out, alive with algae, we would accomplish two things at once: dredging for diatoms and bathing. Nude and solitary, we were the only inhabitants of a world apart, a world of raucous lobos that swam there too, a pair of little penguins uncertain whether to be afraid of us or not, and the millions of piqueros diving at a school of anchobetas farther out. . . .

Svaap in Cherra Bay, Lobos de Tierra, Coast of Peru

Finally we gathered up stuttering Enrique, got in our various mooring lines which held us in place like a spider in its web, for there was no swinging room in the tiny cove, and took up our kedge with a rush as we sailed out over it, gathering momentum as we heeled to the gusts. Again we sailed north along the crashing coast to Albatross Island to photograph its natural arches and its hundreds of lobos, roaring and bleating (for there were babies) all over its cliffs. Every inch was covered, either with lobos or birds, all trying to outdo one another and drown out the roar of the surf. Again past Cape Cross. With a setting sun of passionate Peruvian colours we anchored near the old wreck of the square-rigger. Enrique set out on his weary cold march back to the light. Dan let the galley stove burn longer than necessary, to warm up the cabin. Sooky and Gaynose came out for their evening playtime, joyous and thriving. Gaynose was growing a new thicker coat of fur, which if it was due to the unaccustomed climate was an extra-ordinary example of immediate adaptation of species, but which was more likely a seasonal thing. This particular night Gaynose discovered that he could bark, or whatever it is that a coati mundi does. It was a squirrel sort of noise but louder. He discovered it in the middle of the night and was so intrigued with the new accomplishment that he experimented and learned variations assiduously the entire rest of the night — finally becoming exhausted at sunrise, falling asleep at his usual waking hour.

Finally one day we said farewell to Enrique and

Gregorio and sailed out past the wreck. A few boobies perched on yards, where once white sails spread. We looked forward to Talara again . . . then Galapagos at last!

Monday, March 5th, 9 *p.m.* — All the afternoon we sailed NW. with a breeze from WSW. to W. So the spinnakers came off shortly after leaving the island. All the afternoon the blue stream slipped past bearing hundreds of thousands of ectoplasm-like jellyfish, innumerable small sharks, and great schools of small fish. As evening came on, many of our bird friends from Lobos Island left their fishing in our vicinity and headed for their island home. For us it was already below the southern horizon, so our last bond with Lobos was gone with the birds.

We neared the south coast of Aguja Point, followed its barren reddish hills as night came on. The breeze had freshened astern now, something unusual for these Humboldt nights close to the coast. Our twin spinnakers plus the tris'l are pulling us along with our long growth of weed and barnacles at a pleasantly comfortable five knots. The sea is afire with phosphorescence, exploding into vivid, startling fireworks when we start up a school of fish, or a huge shark. Small night-birds are chirping like chickens. The sky is overcast. We passed a steamer, low and rakish, at 8 p.m. A small sailing fisherman with no lights very close a little later. We have changed watches and Florence has it now, steering our course with everything pulling in our favour. Aguja light bears

SE. now, so we are past the rock that lies a mile offshore to torment coastwise sailormen. So now we can steer N. by W., our course for the night. With the rock past, everything is clear ahead except to watch for boats, and I can sleep without worrying, for Florence has keen night eyes.

This is sailing that brings back memories — the Koro Sea and its blazing fiery trail streaming off astern as we steer always westward . . . the tranquil Java Sea . . . the Indian Ocean . . . they were like this. Good old *Svaap*. She has gone on and on and has lived more than any other boat of her size in the world. And still we drive her farther. I shall retire her in some quiet harbour, perhaps home at Ipswich, at the end of this voyage, and she shall rest the remaining years.

Tuesday, March 6th — More or less calm most of the night in spite of the breezy beginning. Light land wind early part. Sailing along all day with light westerly. Much sail drill with shifting breeze. The virazon is unsettled. Uneventful.

Wednesday, March 7th — Last night we were in great danger and did not realize it until afterward. The Humboldt Current sets north-west here. We allowed for it and steered a little east of our course. Night fell, with mist of fog proportions, over land and sea. The usual night calm. We kept on under power, suspecting nothing, hearing nothing. I felt uneasy and stayed on without calling Florence to relieve me at eight o'clock when my watch ended. Suddenly I felt *Svaap* lift uneasily, changing her motion ever so slightly. It flashed through me that we were in shoal water, with the long swells mounting up to break. I had no reason to believe that we were closer than five miles, but a hunch — or was it *Svaap* herself that warned me? — told me that we were almost on the beach. The wheel spun to port. We ran straight out to sea without stopping the motor to listen for surf. I knew the surf was there without that. I set a new course that would carry us clear of all land. Long afterward Pariñas showed up dead ahead and proved that we had been near shore close to Chira River, where flats extend out some distance. I think we were within a few feet of going aground. When my bearings on Pariñas light showed that we were hardly gaining, doing about two knots *less* than our speed through the water, instead of that much *faster* with the current at our back, the suspicion that had been growing on me was confirmed. The Humboldt Current was temporarily reversed and the rare *Niño* held sway, so that instead of being set *off* the land we had been set directly *on*shore. The *Niño* (the 'Child' current) that once or twice a year, usually in the period from December to possibly April, pushes down from the north, urged by winds, to disturb the northern end of the Humboldt and form a temporary counter-current as far down as Pariñas, or perhaps to Aguja Point, but never much beyond. We had not thought much of the *Niño*, for it is so rare, but we should have known that if it was ever to occur, it would do so just when we were gloating over our fast run, pushed by wind and current. Now, with the current to meet, we did not reach Talara until early morning, creeping in to our old berth and tying up at 5 a.m.

Wreck Bay, Galapagos

CHAPTER XVII

ISLANDS OF ISOLATION

A REDDISH crescent of new moon followed the sun over
the horizon and left a sky full of fantastic cloud forms.
We steered west with the trade in our sails. *Svaap* had
begun her second crossing of the greatest of all oceans.
I lay awake in my bunk, dreaming I could hear the voice
of Florence, singing low to herself at the wheel. In his
tiny after-cabin Dan slept heavily. Soon, at 10 p.m., he
would go on for his night watch. At 2 a.m. I took it
over. There was something rhythmic and peaceful about
our lives. We seemed in step with the universe.

There was everything on board necessary for a stay of
from six months to a year in Galapagos. Beyond that we
did not know. All the ingenuity resulting from my long
experience in loading small craft had been strained in

173

order to pack into the *Svaap* everything that had to go, and still leave room for us to live aboard. What would not go below was lashed on deck in cases. On each side of the companion-way on deck there was a fifty-gallon drum, one of spare petrol and one of kerosene. Elsewhere on deck were an additional two hundred gallons of water and petrol in five-gallon tins. All our regular tanks and breakers were full. The *Svaap* was so deeply loaded that she groaned beneath the load and responded more heavily to the seas than she had ever done before. She felt like a vessel twice her tonnage, which in fact she was at the moment, with her tremendous burden. Her motions were slow and deliberate, like a lazy, half-submerged whale. Ordinarily it would have been folly to put to sea with such a load, but here, where there are no storms or heavy seas, with our destination but six hundred miles away, it was quite safe.

We were one less aboard. In Talara, Gaynose the coati had grown thinner and thinner, with an appetite more ravenous than ever. He evidently had worms, probably from fish which we often found afflicted. The Company doctor believed he could cure him, so with the gay little fellow trotting confidently at our heels we went to the hospital. Gaynose took everything like a hero, including painful injections, trotted out of the operating-room with us, and fell into convulsions and unconsciousness. Later he recovered for a little while and we thought he would live. We carried him tenderly aboard and let him rest on a soft pillow in his box.

But while we were having dinner he died. Later I curled his inquisitive, affectionate long nose under him and covered it with his paws — as he liked to have it in life. We gently buried him in the sea. Poor Gaynose — he who always loved to be full to bursting died with an empty stomach, hungry. Had he lived a week or two he would have been really happy, for we planned to let him run free about our camp in Galapagos. He could have caught small fish in the tidal pools, and trotted at our heels begging for delicacies. We loved him so much that there were tears in our eyes as the cold Humboldt waters closed over his pathetic, thin little body. Even Sooky the bear was quiet and depressed that night. We suddenly hated Talara and could not wait to leave.

Saturday, March 17*th* — Noon position: 3·52 south, 83·13 west. Day's run 127 miles. During the early night the breeze was a little west of south, fresh and chilly, with all our working sails driving us heavily along. I was called early for my 2 a.m. watch, for the wind had worked into the SE. and called for the port spinnaker — the new big one we had made in Talara. The huge sail went up, filled with the steady night wind and set its back to the task. *Svaap* added a knot or two to her speed. The sparkling wake grew broader. I took the wheel from Dan and settled down for my four hours of dreamy solitude, admiring the magnificent new sail that stretched from mast-head to deck and eighteen feet outboard to the end of the spinnaker boom, like a monstrous wing. I was glad of those permanent backstays

our unique rig provided. If the wind drew farther aft
I would put up the starboard spinnaker too. By lashing
the wheel for a moment I could do it myself without
calling anyone on deck. The booms were permanently
rigged outboard, their base in a mast fitting, their outer
end held fast by a lift and fore and aft guys. They were
only unshipped for really bad weather or continued windward work. Sometimes they remained rigged for weeks
on end, even months. If there was a bad roll we simply
lifted the boom ends a little higher to prevent them from
hitting the wave tops. Setting a spinnaker — even the
enormous new one — was a simple task of a few seconds
for one man, at night as well as by day. For cruising
work the two spinnakers were kept at the base of the
mast on deck, each one in its sail-bag with halyard, outhaul, and sheet all made fast. To set either sail one
simply opened the mouth of the bag, hauled on the
halyard, and the big sail slithered up out of the bag,
fold after fold, to the mast-head. Then a heave on the
outhaul which brought the sail out to the end of the
boom, and the sheet was ready to be belayed. Later,
at leisure, the boom could be adjusted to the proper
angle. There was never any awkward shifting of sails
or booms from one side to the other. Booms and spinnakers were a permanent part of the gear of the vessel,
as much so as the fore and aft booms and their respective
sails. Below were a pair of smaller spinnakers to be used
in place of the big ones when the trade blew strong.

When I think of the time and labour wasted on most

small craft in working with spinnakers I groan. There is no reason in the world why all small vessels cannot do as we did when in good weather latitudes. It is the obvious solution for simplifying and making practical the use of spinnakers at sea.

In every way our extraordinary tris'l rig was proving so perfect that there was nothing I would change. Always there was an ideal combination of sails for every condition. We never reefed. That was unnecessary. Merely take off a sail, the big tris'l with its high centre of effort first, then one or two of the others if the weather grew more boisterous. All easily-handled sails of moderate area. She seemed always in balance, under half a dozen combinations of sails. Nowhere was there any chafe — a godsend on long cruises. It was simplicity itself.

At 6 a.m. Florence took the wheel. After washing down the deck and tidying up I turned in and slept soundly until my ten o'clock sight. I had reverted to my old-time easy-going navigation: a ten o'clock morning sight moved ahead and crossed with a meridian sight to give a noon position fix. This was sufficiently accurate except when making landfalls. A small sailing craft, ambling along at five or six knots, does not need more than one fix a day at sea.

We had been taking water temperatures regularly, to trace the effect of the Humboldt Current. Now, suddenly, in mid-morning when we were 110 miles off-shore, it started to rise, either from a dilution of the colder waters of the current as they spread out into the

M 177

Pacific, or because the main body of the west-going current was running more to the north. (The latter proved to be the case from later developments.) At 10 a.m. it was 77° F. Coincidentally with our entering warmer water, our first flying fish came aboard and we saw our first tropic bird.

Sunday, March 18*th* — Noon position 3·11 south, 85·0 west. Day's run 115 miles. This is disappointing for I had anticipated a much better run from our dead reckoning. We seem to have a strange current against us. The water temperature is now 81° F. with many flying fish. Last evening, still reaching along with big spinnaker, tris'l and mizen, before a SE. trade, we steered straight for a heavy bank of clouds, behind which the sun had set. When the wind swung to S. a little later we took off the light sails and put her on all lowers — expecting a squall. But none came, and the wind went back to SE. at midnight and freshened to strong trade in my early morning watch. We have been rolling heavily since then in the correspondingly increased sea.

6 *p.m.* — There is a reverse current here instead of the long-expected north-westerly set from the Humboldt Current. It must be a back eddy or counter-current from the main stream which is probably running in the usual direction but farther north. At 4 p.m. we entered a region of doldrum airs and light rain; lowered all sail to wait for breeze. I always prefer to do this rather than to have the sails banging back and forth, beating the life out of the fabric and weakening the seams. *Svaap*

still headed steadily about NNW. Potato peels drifted steadily astern as Dan prepared for supper. The trolling line streamed out astern as if we were under way. It was obvious that this counter-current was something to be reckoned with. I made a mental note of it in case we had to return to the coast at some later date.

8 *p.m.* — Spinnakers set again, port and starboard. Faint easterly air dead aft, and squalls. Typically doldrum weather. Rain driving all Florence's watch.

Monday, March 19*th* — Sky overcast. No sights. Light rain at times and only light airs from E. and SE. My watch fairly good, no real rain, but when Florence took it the rain came again, killing all breeze. I did not expect to find this weather here and am much disappointed. Port holes over my berth suddenly leak. This should not bother me much, for once in the Galapagos we do not expect rain more than once in a blue moon.

5 *p.m.* — Calms and light rain squalls, with occasional easterly airs. Confused jumpy sea full of current rips. Little progress. Many tropic birds, small sea-swallows, miniature brown jelly-fish with brown stings hanging down beneath, and also countless small organisms floating all over the surface of the sea.

9 *p.m.* — A beautiful fresh breeze came up out of the north of all places (we should be having southerly weather here) and we are bowling along in a lump of a sea, doing five knots beneath a clear sky, with the sinking moon dead ahead as we steer W. by N.

Tuesday, March 20*th* — Noon position 1·58 south,

87·17 west. Distance run in 48 hours since noon of 18th, 159 miles. Only 144 miles to Hood Island. Already the excitement of an expected landfall is upon us. We were going first to Hood Island, to anchor in Gardner Bay. I have never been there before. Last night's breeze stiffened more and more until it was strong trade force, but still right out of the north. Heavy wet going all night under lowers only. No early morning lull in weather as usual. To-day is brilliant, cloudless. Sights are difficult to take because of the motion but managed with fair accuracy. From long practice I am able to snatch a sight just at the moment we hesitate on top of a sea, with no other crests intervening between my telescope and the horizon. I should like to take certain steamship captains who sniff at small boat navigation away from their high wide bridges, steady as dance floors, and let them try a few sights from the deck of *Svaap*, or any other small ocean-going yacht.

Wednesday, March 21st — Noon position 1·47 south, 89·39 west. Distance run 140 miles. The northerly held through the night although not so hard as before. With sunrise it weakened and hauled toward the E. All night we steered south of our course allowing for the northerly set which I experienced among the Galapagos before. This morning we looked ahead in vain where Hood Island should have been. There was only empty ocean. A hastily-worked sight showed that we were far to the south, almost twenty miles too far. We wearily got her close hauled and headed north, cursing the Galapagos for their almost invariable capacity to impede human visitation or habitation. Last voyage, coming from the north, I had fought head winds and current. Remembering, I had deliberately made for Hood Island, the southernmost island, in order to slide up through the group with the current and wind behind us. Now a totally contrary current had upset our nice calculations and we were worse off than ever, having deliberately steered too far south in addition to having been carried there by the unexpected current during the last night. It meant another day and night at sea.

The breeze died in mid-afternoon. We had not as yet sighted the island which lay a few miles to the north of us. Night came on, with a moon in the first quarter and jewels of stars sparkling in a deep purple sky. We started the motor, the first time since leaving Talara, and tried to close with the island before the moonlight failed. The current was too strong. We stopped the motor when the moon set, and still no island, and lay there on the sea, gently moving with the swell. A faint rumble of surf was the only sign that we had at last reached our destination: 'The Enchanted Isles'.

During the night-calm, while we slept, the current set us back again out of sight or sound of the island, so that dawn found us still on an empty ocean. But when the sun rose to level its rays over the sea from the east, to reach at last the northern horizon, they shone on the low pile of the island and disclosed it to us, mantled in a cloak of rose. The slow-moving clouds were reflected in the unruffled waters as they breathed uneasily in restless conflicting swells. The *Svaap* rose and fell, eager to find her first anchorage. The morning breeze came in; our sails fell quiet and leaned to their work. . . .

Hood rose abruptly from the sea in low cliffs, covered with a sparse scrubby green growth. It was our first green for many weeks, for coastal Peru is an unbroken desert. Hood had an un-Galapagos-like appearance, with softer contours, yellow beaches, greens, and no visible cones. Our weeks on the Peruvian coast, with its arid monotony, made this the more welcome. We lunched on deck as we came close to the base of the cliffs, *Svaap* sailing herself with lashed wheel, and gazed upon immense spouts shooting geyser-high in blow-holes as the long southerly swells roared in to meet the lava rock of the island base. The spouts hung high in the air for an impossible length of time, as if reluctant to return to the sea.

Tacking close to the cliffs, heading north, we suddenly entered a different current eddy which carried us rapidly past the point of the island and opened up the north coast to our sight. A dozen mighty frigate birds soared with us, close to mast-heads. They are magnificent flyers, almost like the supreme flyer — the great albatross. We beat along the coast close to several beaches, sailing in transparent emerald water at last. The other two gazed in delight into the depths and experienced the thrills that I remembered so well from long ago, when I too first stared down upon sand and coral and exotic fish —

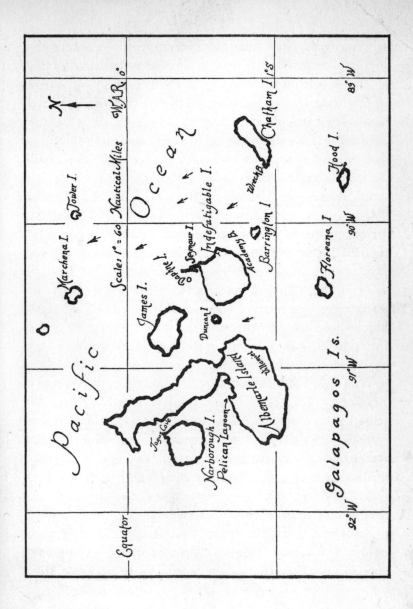

fathoms deep. Now I have a different thrill—a sort of proprietary feeling — as if, by my familiarity with it all, it had become something belonging to me especially. It surges up on the crest of a thousand memories that come rushing back to overwhelm me. And so, as we sailed at last into Gardner Bay, an emerald expanse bounded on the south by blazing beaches separated by black barriers of volcanic rock, and on the north and east by small islets of fantastic design, I was dreaming of Aitutaki, of Bora Bora, and of Mopelia.

Our anchor went down into the sand. Two black fins curled up out of the water nearby, twenty feet apart: a gigantic black bat shape slid along just beneath the surface, coming close. The giant ray circled once. Then, as we brought up on our chain and climbed the rigging for a better view, he emitted a vast cloud of blood-red substance which spread rapidly through the water. Again he circled imperiously — then leisurely went off, leaving his widening bloody cloud behind.

We could hardly wait to get ashore. The canoe was in the water. Our paddles gleamed in the late sun. We neared the beach while a solitary wild goat sauntered by undisturbed along the sand, exactly like some holiday-maker taking a placid sunset stroll. We caught the crest of a wave, rode it up the steep beach and were at last on Galapagos soil, nine months and eleven days after our sweltering departure from Staten Island.

We stood there a moment hesitating, with that queer feeling of a whole teeming world at our finger-tips and uncertainty as to what to do first. We turned east along the shore and came at once upon sea lions. Impertinent Galapagos mocking-birds ran up to our heels and spoke volumes of their excitement at this strange visitation. A pair whom I fed with bananas followed us all the way. Down past the turtle tracks we came upon marine iguanas who ran nimbly into the water and swam among the small breakers that rushed in and out here upon black lava. A school of perhaps a dozen giant rays sported farther out. A few sharks cut the gleaming water with sinister fins. Beyond, boobies plunged recklessly into the sea, to pop out a moment later with another fish in their crops. A homeward-bound booby was chased by a frigate bird, who came after him with long, deliberate, majestic wing-beats, gaining rapidly upon the poor booby whose shorter wings beat with all the speed he could muster. The frigate drove him into the surf, but was defeated, for the booby refused to eject his fish.

The moon rose. We returned to the *Svaap* — we three in the dugout — and no other mortals anywhere in our world. I was full of the wild isolated beauty, still thinking of those nights on the lagoon of Mopelia, when we would go by outrigger to the outer reef to fish. By night the whole bay was still transparent, lit by the moon whose rays reflected from the bottom. The beach was blazing silver; above was the deep purple sky with the Southern Cross over the island. Sea lions roared. A large fish leaped and crashed back. We rolled lazily in a long swell. The trade wind blew gently from the south-east. It was deliciously cool. It had been a proper Galapagos first night.

There was much to tempt us here at Hood but we were anxious to get to work. I had chosen Albemarle as our base. We sailed from Hood the following evening to visit my old acquaintances at Wreck Bay on the island of Chatham. *Svaap* sailed herself all night, rolling along gently at three knots. The night breeze grew faint just before the dawn. . . . I lift my head from the deck where I have been sleeping. We creep through the still black waters silently. I am awake now — all my senses alert — for we have run out our distance to the island. The rattle of blocks as the ship rolls breaks the stillness exasperatingly as I strain to hear the surf. There is a low rumbling. A vague black blur on the eastern horizon — only a shade blacker than the rest — must be Chatham Island. Over it hangs a planet, the brightest star of the whole night, rising about three-thirty and blazing like a tiny sun. A faint light diffuses the east. The blackness begins to fade but the blacker blur stays. The ship quiets her motion as it falls still calmer. The rumble of the surf is plain now: a constant thing that is partly sound and partly feel. The blur takes definite shape gradually, becoming a low pyramid of land. Above, the planet still shines, but behind, the low bank of cloud takes on a deep rose. The clear sky in the semicircle above becomes a graduated blue. In the west it is still night — the deep blue of the sky blends imperceptibly into the sea. The welcome smell of land comes out to us on a cool dawn air. The light sweeps rapidly over the arch of the sky, blotting out star after star until there is only one — the bright planet over the island.

Swiftly the radiant sunrise colours sweep across the east, reflected in overhead wisps of cloud. Suddenly, before I know it has happened, the sea is a vivid polished blue with a million patent-leather ripples dancing merrily over it. The island is real — all its little bumps and hollows are exaggerated by the low rays of the appearing sun. To the left it sweeps down to form Wreck Bay. We steer in for the dilapidated pier, the rusty light structure. The wreck still shows two spars. The half-dozen dingy houses are there still. There is little change in Galapagos in five years.

Karin, the brave Norwegian girl I had known before, is she still here? And Manuel Cobos, whose father was murdered by the convicts? Si! Si! Señor! Karin is married to Señor Cobos now, two children they have! And my honey bear, that I left with Karin five years ago? Si, Señor, it is still there, with Karin up on the mountain, but it is *muy bravo* now.

Cobos came to get us — with horses. We took Sooky along, slung over my shoulder in a big red bandana, to meet his predecessor.

Manuel Cobos rode before us — broad hat, breeches, leather leggings and all — up the familiar dusty red road. Our horses carried us comfortably at a walk. First the typical dry Galapagos growth, cactus, century plant, wild cotton. Higher, greener, denser, yellow blossoms, tiny birds so very tame. A wild-looking vaquero dashing down-hill at a gallop. Higher. Far down, the little bay dented the coastline. There lay *Svaap* again after five years and half a hundred thousand miles. The last rise: the double row of ciruela trees laden with luscious red plum-like fruit.

As we rode we listened to Cobos's tale. He had lost his island kingdom. A company owned the Hacienda and the wild cattle and the horses. They owned the coffee plantations, and the schooner which came occasionally. Cobos had salvaged only a small plantation for himself.

His house stood high on its stilts at the end of a lane. Beyond rose the rolling green hills. Fertility . . . so unexpected and unbelievable to one on the sea coast, but so natural up here among the clouds. El Junco with its crater lake and wild horses. I remembered a fiery red sunset and the wild horses all outlined against the sky along a ridge. Manuel Cobos whistled. Karin ran across a bare wooden floor and stood on the balcony looking strange in a too-formal black silk dress and silk stockings. She was still pretty. But only when she donned riding-clothes and huge sombrero and led us off to ride the plantation did she become the Karin of old. A little heavier. More worldly with the cares of motherhood. But still the Karin of the wild horses, the leaping imagination, and the dream pictures.

Friendships renewed. Reminiscences. And away again — this time to Puerto Grande down the coast, where in an uninhabited cove we careened *Svaap*, and cleaned her bottom of a hoary growth of grass and barnacles. The same cove had been used by the buccaneers for the same purposes long ago. Grown into the roots of very old mangroves we found corroded bits of ancient copper. Perhaps they were fragments from the ships of Dampier, Wafer, or the others.

Then on to Indefatigable — that smoky towering old volcano. There in Academy Bay we called upon the tragic little group of humanity that lives there isolated from the world. There we found Arthur Wörm Muller and his wife Hilda, ageing now: two of the remaining handful of Norwegians connected with the ill-fated colonization scheme which nine years ago brought Karin and the others I had known. They told of the recent death of my friend Captain Bruun who had sailed from Norway to Galapagos in his little *Isabella* at the time of the colonization. Captain Bruun had shared Thanksgiving dinner with me on the *Svaap* five years before, over there in Wreck Bay. I can still taste the delicious turtle soup he made that day from a huge beast we caught in the surf. Now he too was dead, like so many of the others. The sea killed him on the reefs of Albemarle. Nuggerud was there too, another Norwegian, living in a little shack painted all the colours of the rainbow. He was young, strong, and hopeful. He showed me his little fishing boat the *Dinamita* and came to see the *Svaap*. Nuggerud . . . who four months later was dead too — a thirst-parched corpse on the shore of lonely barren Marchena, a hundred miles to the north, with the broken *Dinamita* out there on the reef. Dead beside him was Lorenz, the last of the trio made notorious by the self-styled Empress of Charles Island, the Baroness Eloise Bosquet de Wagner Wehrborn, of Paris and Vienna. The Baroness and her friend had already disappeared, no one knew where, nor did anyone in the islands care. The Norwegian, Stampa, who fished for his livelihood was still in Academy Bay, very busy just now cleaning a huge Galapagos tortoise shell to use as a cradle for the son his wife promised him in a few days. It would be the first baby born there. Doctor? Midwife? Stampa himself would do what he could to help when her time came. This was Galapagos. The Dane, Rader, and Finnsen the Icelander, completed the little band of exiles from the north. Strange how these people from the other end of the earth, from the cold Scandinavian lands, should have chosen these inhospitable islands under the very equator itself for their exile. The urges of man are strange but Fate is stranger yet.

And here, where the entire population could be counted on a man's fingers, was also that poison of social rivalry, envy, and jealousy — more intense than in Talara because more closely confined. I suppose, human nature being what it is, it must exist to some extent in all small isolated communities, in direct ratio to the smallness of the place and the smallness of the people. But to find it rankling here on Indefatigable in Galapagos, to find it here so virulent that one family with higher social pretensions than the others was not on speaking terms with the lesser fry ... it is almost beyond belief. Even this, however, was a mild and harmless manifestion compared with that preposterous situation over on Charles (Floreana) Island, where the population was a scant half-dozen.

Academy Bay was a depressing place. The air seemed thick and unhealthy, foreboding. The mosquitoes filled the air in droves. We hastened on to Albemarle.

CHAPTER XVIII

THE BARONESS AND THE CORPSES

FOR two or three years there have been recurring news accounts of a sensational nature concerning one Galapagos Island in particular: Floreana — otherwise known as Charles, or Santa Maria — a smallish island in the south central part of the group. The popular newspapers and magazines have referred to it as the Eden island, Utopia, Pacific Paradise, Island of Love, and so forth. Floreana is far from any of these. It is a typical Galapagos island of the semi-fertile type, only 26 miles in circumference and less than 1,800 feet in altitude. Its lower slopes and shores are lava country, with a sparse growth of cactus, stunted grey bushes and dwarfed trees. It rarely rains down here. Water is at a premium. Higher up there are fertile regions, with water not quite so scarce but still to be guarded carefully. Up here in the hills there are wild cattle, burros, and goats. At sea level it is impossible to raise even the barest necessities of life. Even in the more fertile areas higher up it is a grim strnggle to grow enough to live on. In short it is a far cry from even a mediocre sort of Garden of Eden. The same *dénouement* applies to the rather sordid handful of strange people who choose to isolate themselves here and who came to be known by the romantic titles of Adam and Eve of the Galapagos; the Mad Empress of the Islands, and her court, living their 'tropic idyll of love' in beautiful retirement (accompanied by every ounce of notoriety that could be squeezed out of it).

Recently the disappearance of the principals, and the finding of two corpses on Marchena Island, 160 miles to the north, brought the whole thing to a sensational climax, and what is undoubtedly a definite Finis — although the actual fate of two and the relation between the various episodes was still shrouded in mystery at the end. The key to the whole thing has for some strange reason been missed or avoided. I have never seen such an incoherent jumble of conflicting facts, obvious impossibilities, and misinformation as was abroad at this time. Perhaps the explanation is in the isolation of the place, and the difficulty of communication. I too am equally remote, writing this under my wide pandanus thatch roof in Tahiti, with the lagoon, the rumbling reef, and the fantastic peaks of Moorea spread before me. Thus *my* alibi for any inaccuracies that may follow. But I have before me (besides countless newspaper clippings on the subject and a knowledge of the islands and the people) letters from various inhabitants of the Galapagos holding the key to the mystery. Also, I was in the islands myself when the last tragic act was being played. So I feel that I may as well play detective too, and offer what I believe is the true story of the Baroness and the corpses. In so doing I may as well go back to the beginning.

The Ritters were not active participants in our little drama of love, jealousy, hatred and death — although Dr. Ritter is dead now too — but they belong to the story as background. When I visited Floreana first, in December of 1928, there were only three human beings on the island: a Norwegian called Urholt, a survivor of one of the ill-fated colonization schemes of which I and others have written elsewhere, and his two Ecuadorean peons. They were engaged in making 'bacalau', an excellent sun-dried fish. Urholt was ready to leave the island for good, waiting for a boat to take him off. Later the island was inhabited temporarily by two or three others who came to hunt for meat in the hills, or to fish. But these were merely transients. The first real settlers on Floreana in modern times were the Ritters, as they were called.

About the time I was roaming the upper slopes of Floreana in 1928 stalking wild pig for my meat supply for the voyage to Tahiti, Dr. Friedrich Ritter, a middle-aged Berlin dentist, was discovering a kindred soul in Frau Dore Koerwin who was one of his patients. Dr. Ritter had strange ideas about life for a staid German dentist. Perhaps I should not say strange, though, for it is not unusual for the professional man to have a wider streak of imagination and interest in the unusual, than the industrialist or man of commerce. About him Ritter saw the German people flocking to the nudist camps that were spreading over the land. There was a country-wide rage for nature fads, new strange diets, exercises . . . a mass groping for a natural life but in an unnatural, erratic, unsystematic way. If *he* were going to do it he would go the whole way — perhaps to some tropical island where he could discard clothing without the mass exhibitionism of the nudist camps, where he could live on vegetables and fruits that he would grow himself, working in the open air and sun . . . why if he could do that — live an entirely natural life — he could probably double the span of years allotted to man! But he would want companionship, and his wife laughed at his ideas. Frau Koerwin listened sympathetically. Before long they had decided to burn their bridges behind them and make the experiment together. Dr. Ritter, knowing professionally the painful results of neglected teeth, had all his extracted. He made himself a set of stainless steel. These should last him forever. With the perversity of notoriety these teeth became the outstanding fact known about Dr. Ritter by the outside world. Instead of his revolutionary ideas on life, his courage in applying them, Dr. Ritter became known as the man with the steel teeth. There was nothing extraordinary about these teeth in appearance, however, for contrary to general belief they were coated with enamel and appeared not unlike other sets. Dore Koerwin kept her own teeth, for he could take care of hers when they gave trouble. He said good-bye to his wife; Frau Koerwin to her husband, a stiff Berlin gymnasium professor. In 1929, some months after *Svaap* sailed into the west from Floreana, Dr. Ritter and his former patient arrived with that small equipment they believed necessary to live there for the rest of their lives. They became the Adam and Eve of the Galapagos. Why they chose the Galapagos I do not know. They could hardly have found a more unsuitable place unless it was their idea that the very grimness and severity of the struggle necessary to produce a meagre living in the decidedly inhospitable spot they chose, would perfect their health. In any case they cast off their clothes and built themselves a shelter by a trickle of water a half-hour inland from Black Beach, moved tons of boulders from a small area that was to be their garden and planted their seeds. Unforeseen difficulties were constantly cropping up: the birds ate their seeds and their fruit, their water supply had to be constantly conserved, the mosquitoes and prickly bushes were severe on nudists. But they were full of ingenuity and determination and stuck it out like the serious people they were.

Next came the Wittmers, another German couple, with their half-blind son in his teens. Later there was a baby. They were more prosaic in their ideas and did not catch the popular fancy as did the Ritters. Hence not so much is known about them. They were seeking their particular form of escape also, though in a more conventional manner. They settled far enough away from the Ritters so that they were not in each others' way. Soon they also were unobtrusively arranging their own lives.

Such was the peaceful setting (peaceful in spite of friction which soon developed between the Ritters and the Wittmers) on Floreana in the first part of 1932. It was not to remain so for long, for there had already arrived in Guayaquil on the mainland a flashing young woman, a 'dark-eyed beauty' known as the Baroness Eloise Bosquet de Wagner Wehrborn, formerly of Vienna and Paris. With her were two male companions, Alfred Rudolph Lorenz, her lover, and Robert Phillipson, a friend, both German. She soon set the town agog with rumours of a project to make a world summer-resort in the Galapagos, plans to build a hotel there, and to have the islands become a regular port of call for the Grace Line ships. In August of that year she sailed for the islands with her men and arrived on Floreana, settling not far from the Wittmers. The island then and there lost whatever peaceful Eden-quality it may have had and became overcrowded and hectic. It leaped recurringly through the news in a series of sensational episodes

centring around the Baroness, or the 'Empress' as she
had now become, for upon her arrival she had declared
herself ruler of the island. Tolerating the presence of the
other two establishments, she proceeded to exercise her
authority upon stray visitors to the island, resenting their
intrusion by confining them, driving them away, or even
shooting them. Discretion prevailed, however, when
visiting yachtsmen called, and she was then to a certain
extent even hospitable. But the less influential visitors
continued to be met with something different. She
affected an abbreviated costume of brassière and silk
shorts, with a pistol which she was only too quick to use
hanging from her waist. A young Dane from one of the
other islands joined her retinue and when he wanted to
leave was shot in the abdomen by the Baroness, not
fatally. One Pablo Rolando and Blanco Rosa his bride,
shipwrecked on their honeymoon voyage and stranded
on the island, were cast adrift again in a small open boat.
Fortunately they were picked up later by a fishing craft,
and lived to tell their tale to the Ecuadorean authorities.
There was a rumour that one of her 'subjects', possibly an
Ecuadorean peon, was shot to death. There was ill-
feeling with the Wittmers, whose presence she resented
and who returned the feeling. Her strange mania took
other forms. She would shoot animals and nurse them
well again. Norwegians who came from Academy Bay
to shoot fresh meat in the hills were driven off. While
in Academy Bay, my friend Stampa the Norwegian told
me how he had been shot at by the Baroness when he had

gone to Floreana for meat. The island was hers, she decreed, and she was there to prove it.

Her domestic affairs were equally disturbing. Instead of the highly romanticized 'love idyll' described in the papers, life among the three was a festering sex complex culminating in a series of brawls as the men fought with each other and the woman cast off her lover Lorenz and took on Phillipson. The quarrels and struggles (which became journalistic 'daily duels of strength between the two knights for the favour of their queen, who watched and urged them on') could have only one conclusion, for Lorenz was too small and weak to be a match for the other. Thus Lorenz was reduced to a sort of 'super-scullion' — a slave to the other two. Once Lorenz was beaten so badly that he took shelter with the Wittmers for several months. He told my friend Arthur Wörm Muller of Academy Bay, when he called in at Post Office Bay one day during this period, that he had 'barely escaped with his life'. Later, strangely enough under the circumstances, he returned to the tyrannous establishment of the Baroness, perhaps with a plan in mind. In any case all went well for a time, until on March 28, 1934 (some versions say the 23rd,) the Wittmers heard another uproar from their neighbours. Going to investigate, they say that they found Lorenz standing wild-eyed by the deserted, disordered shack. There had been a fight, he is said to have explained, and the Baroness and Phillipson had gone off 'on an American yacht'.

Lorenz too had now had enough, it seems, and wrote

letters to his brother in Germany, yearning to return, asking that money to enable him to do so be sent to him at Guayaquil. His earlier letters had told of his being cast off by the Baroness and of his fights with Phillipson. Lorenz very distraught and anxious to leave, could only put a notice in the Post Office Bay mail barrel, asking to be taken off by the first boat that came there. Then he sat down nervously to wait. One day the little *Dinamita* came from Academy Bay, with Nuggerud her owner, and his deckhand. They found Lorenz's note in the barrel. When they left they took Lorenz with them, at last on the first lap of his long journey home.

The next scene in the drama takes place four months later, on the tiny barren island of Marchena, 160 miles to the north of Floreana, far isolated from the main body of the Galapagos Islands. It was late afternoon, November 17, 1934. The *Santa Amaro*, one of the little fleet of American fishermen that often cruise as far south as the Galapagos in quest of the fat juicy tuna, swung in to anchor off Marchena. Something on shore caught their eye — a pole with fluttering remnants of tattered fabric. A white object nearby. A boat was manned and the skipper went ashore. They found an improvised signal mast — and an overturned skiff without oars or rowlocks. From beneath the skiff protruded a human body. A few steps away they found another corpse, its head on a pile of clothes, a white coat over its face. Both were badly decomposed. Near the bodies they found a number of letters from people in Academy Bay and in Floreana, a bundle of baby clothing, and a little French money. There was a dead seal, with pieces of meat hacked from it, and remnants of iguana. A small pile of wood and charred paper with burnt matches completed the tragic little setting that told its story so graphically. There was no note explaining what had happened, and only one clue to identity: a German passport with the name of Alfred Rudolph Lorenz.

Back aboard the *Santa Amaro* the wireless chattered away, calling the Mackay wireless station in Los Angeles, to tell what had been found. Soon the story was on the press. Eager editors looking up their files on Galapagos doings, and consulting various people who had been in the islands, concocted fantastic theories as to the corpses. The contents of the letters added to the available store of information. Anyone's theory was as good as the next man's.

The captain of the *Santa Amaro* thought the bodies were Lorenz's and Wittmer's, and had a long complicated theory to explain why.

One news service had it that they were the Wittmers, 'tired of their Eden and looking for a new island to settle on'.

Another claimed that the Baroness and Phillipson had at last been found.

Stampa also was said to be one of the bodies . . . Stampa who was once shot at and captured by the Baroness.

It was even said that it was Dr. Ritter. And that it was Lorenz and Nuggerud, banished at pistol point in a small boat without food and water by the 'Mad Empress of the Galapagos', forgetting that the 'Empress' and her last lover had preceded Lorenz in their disappearance from Floreana.

Both the skipper of the *Santa Amaro* and members of his crew are quoted as hinting darkly of the contents of the letters they found, of 'things that happened on Floreana too horrible for us to imagine'. I believe I have one or two of those letters in my possession. What the men of the *Santa Amaro* referred to is no doubt the accusation of murder contained therein.

The various theories were gradually disposed of. Phillips Lord wirelessed from at sea, *en route* from Galapagos to Tahiti, that he had dined with the Wittmers the week before. That let them out. Gradual checking up on what had happened in the Galapagos and who was missing eliminated most of the false identifications. Confused readers finally learned, if they still cared, that the one thirst-wracked body was undoubtedly Lorenz, the cast-off lover of the Baroness, and that the other was probably Nuggerud, the Norwegian from Academy Bay who had rescued Lorenz from his Paradise which had become Purgatory.

Thus the mystery of the disappearance of the Baroness and Phillipson, and of the corpses on Marchena. All that is needed is the explanation of it all. I think that explanation is obvious.

Peace had returned to Floreana now that the 'Empress had vanished to the South Seas'. Mrs. Wittmer wrote that 'conditions are peaceful, now that our overbearing

neighbour has gone'. She had not loved her missing neighbour too well, and did not stress too much her inexplicable departure. All sounded well — except for certain disturbing letters that Dr. Ritter now wrote to his friends in America. The Ritters had kept severely to themselves and had escaped any embroilment in the recent trouble. Now Dr. Ritter wrote: 'We hope you will come back to the islands. Then I will tell you what I cannot write because I have no proof'. One of the Americans to whom Dr. Ritter wrote did come back to the islands soon afterwards. But he found Dr. Ritter already dead, of a stroke his Eve said, his secret gone with him into his shallow grave. Dore Koerwin returned soon after to Germany, where she is said to be writing a book about it all.[1]

Another Galapagos settler wrote to me from Academy Bay after the disappearance of the Baroness: 'The Baroness and sweetheart have disappeared — no one knows where — they may have been killed'.

I have still another letter before me, more explicit:

'I suppose you have read of the tragedies on the Galapagos Islands, only it seems to me that the American newspapers are of the opinion that the Baroness went away. We down here that know the conditions on the islands believe differently. First it would be almost impossible for a vessel to arrive there without anybody else seeing it, and besides if the Baroness had gone away she would have taken her clothes and other personal belongings, and

[1] *Satan came to Eden* (1936)

everything was left behind. Also Lorenz and Wittmer started pulling down her house, and removed it and everything else to Wittmer's house a few days after her disappearance, something they would not have dared to do *if they had not known for certain that she would never come back*, as both the Wittmers and Lorenz were her bitter enemies. Everyone believes Lorenz guilty. But did he commit the crime alone? Nobody suspects Dr. and Mrs. Ritter. They were nice people even if they had queer ways. Dr. Ritter's sudden death is also a mystery. Mrs. Ritter went back to Germany, where she is to finish and publish a book of Dr. Ritter's. She is also writing one herself.'

The same letter had news of the *Dinamita* and the homeward-bound Lorenz. They had come from Floreana to Indefatigable, where the people in Academy Bay had talked with them. Lorenz was impatient to get to Guayaquil and persuaded Nuggerud to take him on to Chatham to catch the island schooner which was leaving Wreck Bay soon for the mainland. They 'left Academy Bay for Chatham on 13th of July. They were seen in the distance off Chatham the next morning but never arrived. They were never heard from again'. . . . So near were they to safety — and Lorenz to a life haunted by the memory of what happened on Floreana. For Lorenz, it can now be confidently asserted, killed the Baroness and the man who had ousted him from her favour. He may have had an accomplice, but I doubt it.

That the Baroness and Phillipson left Floreana on an

American yacht is, as the letter says, out of the question. Either the Ritters or the Wittmers would surely have known of the presence of a yacht. Besides, the *Svaap* was the only American yacht (or any kind of a yacht at all) in the islands at that time. On the 28th of March, the date the Baroness is supposed to have gone, the *Svaap* was serenely anchored in Wreck Bay and we were in the hills at Progresso, with Cobos and Karin. Even so the *Svaap* was for a long while (unknown to us, as was the disappearance of the Baroness itself) thought to have been the vehicle for the disappearance. A little juggling of dates by the press had us leaving Wreck Bay March 27th (instead of April 5th as we did) 'having had to pass by Floreana on the 28th day of March! Can this be coincidence?' In Guayaquil they did not learn until eight months later that this theory was impossible. On December 11th Captain Hancock came to Tagus Cove on the *Velero III* on a Galapagos expedition, and wirelessed that the *Svaap* was in Tagus Cove. This 'meant the elimination of the only means the Empress of the Galapagos might have had for her fantastic and mysterious departure from Floreana!' said the Guayaquil paper, coming closer to the point than most of the American papers.

Even supposing the Baroness had gone away on some yacht not known to be in the Galapagos at the time, which stopped only long enough to take them on board and sail away — obviously out of the question — then the departing couple would have taken at least some of their possessions with them. Furthermore, the Baroness is no woodland flower, hiding modestly from the world. Had she gone away as is claimed, her flare for notoriety would surely have brought news of her by now.

It is impossible to say what actually happened, but I am inclined to think that Lorenz, during the period when he took refuge with the Wittmers after having been beaten nearly to death, brooding over his troubles and mistreatment, consumed with hatred, conceived his revenge. Simulating forgetfulness, he returned to the fold, took up his distasteful duties of waiting on the arrogant two, biding his time. When an opportune moment came he killed them, probably at night while they were sleeping. Either one of the others was more than a match for him, so he would be taking no chances. Whether he had help or not is doubtful. Probably not. Most likely he disposed of the bodies soon after the crime, removed any traces of what had happened, and waited until later in the day to call the Wittmers. The latter say they ran to investigate a loud disturbance and found Lorenz there, wild-eyed, alone. The Baroness and Phillipson had just left on the mythical American yacht. It is inconceivable that the Wittmers, hearing this, would not have rushed to the shore to see the yacht. The Wittmers knew as well as Lorenz that there was no yacht there, so they must have known then, if they had not already known it, what had happened to the missing lovers. As my Galapagos correspondent writes, they and Lorenz would not have dared to remove the personal belongings, the house and everything, had they not known for certain that the Baroness would never come back. I do not blame the Wittmers for keeping silent, for protecting Lorenz as they were doing, not knowing that he would soon be beyond need of protection in this world. Anyone familiar with the events leading up to it knows that the Baroness and Phillipson had it coming to them. The wonder is that it did not happen sooner.

I think the only doubt remaining is what Lorenz did with the bodies. He could have done several things. He could have buried them or hidden them somewhere nearby in a crevice in the rocks, in which case they will some day be found. He could have dragged them to the sea and let the sharks dispose of them. Or he could have put them into a small boat and sent them to sea by the never-failing current that sweeps past the island. This last possibly sounds far-fetched. My only reason for suggesting it is because a small boat was missed from the island about this time. This suggests perhaps that the missing two might have used it to go away in. Obviously, had they wished to commit suicide they might have done this, but then there would have been no reason for the fiction of the American yacht, nor would Lorenz have dared to strip and demolish the house, for they might have changed their minds and returned. So I think that beyond any doubt the Baroness and her paramour died in return for the degradation and cruelty to which they subjected Lorenz, the under-dog, or to change the simile, the worm who absorbed his cup of humiliation to the dregs and turned.

The final chapter in the life of Lorenz, the rejected lover, will never be known with certainty. His nervous flight from the islands was in reality a haunted effort to escape from his crime. My friends in Academy Bay saw him leave on July 13th for Chatham in the *Dinamita* with the unfortunate Nuggerud. They took the little package of mail from Floreana and a few letters from Academy Bay. Also the bundle of baby clothes which was found by them later, probably for Karin who was soon to have a little daughter. They were sighted from Chatham next morning. Then the veil of uncertainty falls upon the rest of the story. The *Dinamita* at best was a very undependable craft. She had often gone out of commission before, always in a fortunate place heretofore. Probably her engine again broke down. Possibly Nuggerud miscalculated and had not quite enough fuel. In any case, when the sun rose over the peak of El Junco that morning, and the wild horses came to drink in the crater lake, the men in the little boat out there, with their goal just out of reach, began their last journey, carried day and night to the north by the relentless current, growing hungrier and thirstier until they came within reach of Marchena. Lorenz knew then that he was to pay the penalty in full for his crime, and with interest.

Somewhere the *Dinamita* disappears, possibly on the reefs jutting out from Marchena itself, and the men are in the skiff. They have enough strength to drag the skiff out of reach of the tide. But even before they set foot on Marchena they know their Fate. For there is no water there. They hope feebly for the miracle of a passing vessel and put up the pole with the rags on it to attract attention. At first they kill iguanas, and a seal or two, and drink the blood. They cannot achieve a fire so they eat some of the meat raw. It makes them violently ill. Possibly a tuna boat passes in the distance and hope returns for a flickering moment. Then empty ocean again, with the blistering sun creeping overhead a few times. Fever runs into delirium which fades into kindly Death.

And that is all I can tell you of the Baroness and the corpses.

CHAPTER XIX

ALBEMARLE

ALBEMARLE — the greatest of the Galapagos Islands —
stretches more than a degree of latitude from north to
south. Its vast bulk is made up of five great volcanoes
joined together by impassable reaches of crumbling,
caving lava, herculean cinders, impenetrable scrub brush
in the limited areas where it is possible for even this
seemingly lifeless vegetation to live. A handful of people
glean a precarious existence in one spot on the southern
side: Villamel. And Señor Gil has his plantation up above
the village of that name — which consists of a half-dozen
shacks — in one of the meagre areas of fertility that occur

in the higher altitudes. For the rest, Albemarle is uninhabited and uninhabitable.

We circled the majestic pile to the western coast, which for a considerable area is protected by mountainous Narborough across the strait. This region, south of Tagus Cove, the most isolated part of the Galapagos, was rich in the animal and bird life we had come to study. We anchored in several places and explored the coast by canoe. The latter now had an outrigger like the ones in Polynesia and had become a very seaworthy little craft, necessary for this work in the everlasting surf of Galapagos shores. For days we combed the coast, until we found the spot most suited to our purpose. It was an uncharted little cove, near Elizabeth Bay. We named it Pelican Lagoon after its grotesque inhabitants. At the entrance lay a tiny island with a large mangrove tree that was inhabited all day long by climbing black marine iguanas three feet long. We named it Iguana Tree Island, and the inlet to our lagoon became Iguana Tree Inlet.

Having chosen our base we left and went to Tagus Cove, a day's sail to the north. There we erected our Post Office — a large canvas-covered box fastened to a small tree. Tagus Cove is occasionally visited by American tuna fishing vessels from California, and by passing yachts. We had arranged in Panama to have our mail left for us in this manner in Tagus Cove. We planned to come every few weeks to visit our Post Office, and to leave outgoing mail. We lay in Tagus Cove a day or so. As luck would have it we met there a tuna boat, the *Santa*

Cruz from San Diego. They were in for a night only, and then left for the north, to fill their ice-packed hold with fat juicy tuna. Our work done, we hoisted sail and headed south once more for our anchorage off Pelican Lagoon.

We were settling down to stay. This was to be our base for many months. I decided to build a permanent camp ashore, in the location we had chosen on Pelican Lagoon. We loaded the canoe to the gunwales — even the outrigger float was heavily piled with gear — and when we climbed gingerly on top of the load the wavelets were lapping over the edges. Having lived among the Polynesians for two years and more, I have endless confidence in canoes. The other two were more than a little surprised though, when we made shore still afloat.

Soon we were established as Galapagos residents. We put up a shelter tent of an old sail and our spinnaker booms. Our tent was at once adopted by a pair of vivid little lava lizards who always thereafter shared our lunch crumbs when we ate ashore. Our wild neighbours, generally, accepted us without fear or hesitation. Our special pelican friend who always sat in a tiny mangrove bush, swaying and tottering grotesquely, would not bother to fly, even though we tied our canoe to his very branch. The pelicans seemed to choose the most ridiculous roosts, in harmony with their appearance and actions, preferring small shaky branches that will barely support their heavy cumbersome bodies. One in particular acquired a mad desire to alight on my head. I was constantly dodging him as we came by in the outrigger. Whether or not this was a subtle pelican insinuation as to my personal appearance I do not know.

In any case it is not without precedent, for Lionel Wafer, who spent considerable time in the Galapagos with the buccaneers two hundred and fifty years ago, records similar experiences with the bird life of the islands: 'At this Island (identity uncertain) there was but one Watering place, and there we Careened our Ship. Hither many Turtle-Dove and other Birds resorted for Water; which were at first so familiar with us, that they would light upon our Heads and Arms; insomuch that for several Days we maintained the Ship's Company with them. . . .'

As we paddled in the lagoon the large marine iguanas, who look like and are descendants of prehistoric reptiles, hardly interrupted their leisurely swimming in the quiet waters, or their industrious feeding on the tough moss-like growth that was exposed when the tide was out. When frightened while in the water they would dive and swim under the surface with a rippling motion, their legs held close to their bodies. Certain individuals had regular all-day sunning places. There was in particular the grand-father of them all who always spent the day sunning him-self on a particular branch of the mangrove tree on our island. He had many relations and descendants who draped themselves over other desirable branches until it be-came a crazy fairy-story kind of tree, laden with grotesque fruit. Every evening at dusk a solitary frigate bird came floating regally out of the sky, circling and planing over-head, lower and lower, until he settled on a comfortable

Marine Iguanas

fork in the same tree and slept there the night through. A tall dignified crane who lived nearby became more and more intimate, until he finally came and fished each day in our own tide pool, in order to watch our curious actions more closely.

Our real pet, however, was a little stoop-shouldered discouraged-looking bird built somewhat like a penguin and about the same size. He wore a beautiful mottled golden-brown coat, and was probably some sort of night heron. When he was not busy stalking small fry along the water's edge with a Sherlock Holmes air he would come and stand close to our feet hunched up in the most dejected position, as if he carried the burden of the world upon his little round shoulders. He had a mate who was more timid, and who would perch on the safe other-side of the inlet, calling for him to return, which he never did while we were there.

When we wanted fresh fish we first found a crab or two on shore before returning to *Svaap*. A little of the white meat on a hook would catch a small fish of some sort and this in turn would be our bait for bottom fishing for larger edible fish. We brought up many weird creatures of all shapes and colours, some of them quite good to eat but none that compared with the more gamey fish we liked so much — the tuna, the dolphin, and the mackerel. These fish responded to more manly bait and spurned unsporting bottom fishing. They preferred the rush and excitement of chasing their food along the surface or out into the air in a flash of spectrum-breaking colour. So when we tired of bottom fish we sailed out across the bay and trolled until we caught a fat brutish tuna, twenty or thirty pounds of solid delicious flesh. We never lacked fresh fish and nearly always preferred it to our tinned meat. The jaunty little grey lava gulls were with us all the time without fear, perching on the rail chattering among themselves. When a fish was caught they would become tremendously excited, sitting next to us or on our knees to get the scraps, chortling over their good luck with crowlike laughter.

Sooky, our bear, grew fatter by the day. He played more than ever before and was exuberantly happy. I had built him a home in a small round beer barrel with a hinged door in front. At night when we wanted to sleep we stowed him away in this. In the morning, the minute any one of us stirred, Sooky would set his signal going and would not stop until he was let out. Then he would eat a banana or two and make a bee-line for the forward ventilator, his favourite means of ingress, through which he would lower himself by his tail for his morning playtime. After hiding from us behind pillows, chewing on corks, and carrying on a minute exploration of the cabin, he would tire and disappear up forward to sleep all day in a dark locker by the stem of the boat. Sooky, being a Panamanian kinkajou, or honey bear, is a nocturnal, sleeping through the day but awakening instinctively at dusk. Sooky's best hours were in the evening when we returned to the *Svaap*. He would just be awaking, and would stuff himself with bananas and oatmeal until he was nearly as round as the barrel he lived in. Then he would play on deck and below until we were ready for bed when he would be put in his barrel. When awake he was the perfect example of perpetual motion always wanting to play, chewing on our fingers or toes, getting himself into an endless succession of comical attitudes. Every gesture, every move and expression, were just what one would expect of a toy teddy bear could it come to life. *Svaap* would have seemed dreary without him.

Every day we went ashore and worked, photographing the wild life near our camp. It was strenuous work. Lava, and volcanic ejections, make the world's worst surface. When there were no clouds, the reflected heat was withering. Our work, however, was so engrossing that our interest held steadily at peak. Days and then weeks had passed, but our enthusiasm was stronger than ever.

On Sundays we had a rest from our work ashore. It was not a holiday for we each had duties before we could relax. Dan would have a clean-up in the galley, his department, and hurry ashore to paint. I would go over the engine, and other odd jobs, and write my notes. Florence did the week's washing, which, even though we wore but few clothes, was a job. She was allowed but one pail of fresh water. Rinsing was done in salt water. There were always repairs to our clothing and to our shoes, which suffered terribly from the vicious clutch of the lava. During my previous stay in Galapagos I found heavy gym shoes with thick rubber soles and canvas tops to be the best footgear. They do not slip on lava, and they stand the slashing wear better than anything else, for the rubber is soft enough to cushion the knifelike edges of the lava without cutting, and the tops can be repaired with canvas and a sail-needle. Even the heaviest leather shoes or boots are short-lived, for they are easy prey to the jagged lava. Metal studs or plates on the soles are dangerous, for they slip on lava and a fall is apt to be fatal.

I found time to do some reading, from our library of more than two hundred volumes, mostly related to the things we love: exploration and discovery, primitive races and isolated islands. In off moments I would be far away planning new voyages, letting my imagination run under the stimulus of a world chart. Or I would work on the plans for the new *Svaap*. Every man who sails the seas in little ships has his dream ship which he hopes some day to build. Mine is near completion . . . on paper, with every little detail of hull, rig, and layout thought out with infinite care and drawn to scale — ready for the day when she may become an actuality. There is so much to be done in life, and so little time. All my life I have found the days and years too short. I do not fear death very much, but there is such a lot to do before. I cannot comprehend being bored with life. No matter how exciting to-morrow is going to be, there is much to do to-day.

CHAPTER XX

WILD DOGS

WE were hard at work one day near our camp making photographic studies of the iguanas. Suddenly we heard distant cries. It was startling and eerie. We stood motionless while a pack of wild dogs came into sight, hunting toward us along the broken shore. Once they stopped to kill an iguana, ate him on the spot, and came on, yelping and baying back and forth. They had never seen humans. They probably mistook us, standing rigid there, for part of the scenery — a new kind of cactus perhaps. They were splendid beasts, tan and white, something like a smallish Great Dane, with heavy heads and jaws, powerful legs and feet. There were four: a large male, his mate, and two half-grown pups. They were almost at our feet, their noses sniffing the ground puzzled at our scent. I moved and spoke to them. The sudden blank amazement in their eyes as they froze in their tracks told a story. Fear swept over them like a cloud and they ran, panic-stricken. The pups whimpered pitifully as they scampered off, trying to keep up with the old pair and yet not tear their feet on the lava. I looked about me and saw our peefer bird close by, some iguanas a step or two from my feet, all unconcerned, and the anomaly of this land struck me more forcibly than ever before — this land where the wild animals are tame but the tame ones are wild.

This was the first chapter of our wild dog experience. They developed a fatal curiosity. Perhaps it was a vague urge passed on to them by other generations now dead, generations who had lived with men. For their ancestors must have come on ships from another world than this, from South America with the Spanish, or from America with the whalermen, or possibly, even, from the ships of the buccaneers.

Every day they came picking their way along the shore from the north. They would swing around in a wide semicircle to a ridge, from which they would watch. But never did they dare come near. They must have stayed within a mile or so of us always, for their travel across the terrible lava was painful to say the least. Their presence proved to us that there was water somewhere near although our careful search had not discovered it. Nearly every day rain clouds wrapped themselves around the mountains and we could see squalls up there that must have poured quantities of water upon the inhospitable slopes. The dogs had evidently found some outcropping of this lower down, or perhaps pools in the lava.

Then one day we had welcome visitors. The yacht *Stranger* came to our bay. When her owner, Fred Lewis, learned of the dogs he was eager to get one of the pups to take back. We joined forces and cornered them one day on Iguana Tree Island where they often swam to hunt iguanas, as was their custom. I caught one of the pups with a long handled landing-net and when the *Stranger* left next day he was aboard, with comfortable surroundings and plenty of good food for the first time in his life. The dogs had fled.

We returned to our work ashore. At noon the dogs came. They were changed animals — no longer the cringing, skulking creatures that had spied upon us daily from their distant ridge. They had cast off their fear and marched in a compact band to our tent where we were resting from the sun, having a bite of chocolate and ship's biscuit. There they stood, facing us, demanding their missing pup with determined barks and growls. We drove them off but they stayed near by all day. Next day they came closer. They were evidently determined to get the pup back at all costs. They could easily have torn us to pieces. It began to be an ugly situation.

Four days later saw the climax. Dan was doing some painting. Florence and I took the canoe. We heard the dogs baying from early morning. We approached the landing-place. There they stood, on the lava at the water's edge, the male and the bitch, with the half-grown pup. They spelled defiance in every fibre. We decided to call their bluff. I was loath to injure them, not believing it would be necessary. I stepped ashore in front of them, brandishing my paddle and shouting. For the moment their original fear cowed them and they started away. We tied the canoe and went toward our camp. With a renewal of courage the dogs made a rush — abandoning all caution with the last vestiges of fear. We barely reached the canoe in time.

It was an almost unbelievable situation. We, the lords of the earth, hunted by wild dogs! I have never known dogs very well or perhaps I might not have been so amazed. But I had never dreamed that animals could feel so strongly the loss of their young. I would have expected resistance, fury, at the time of the theft — but this deliberate determined campaign of theirs, culminating in actual attack days after the loss, was something inconceivable. I now had to realize that no matter how repugnant the thing was I had no alternative but to kill them, or give up our work in this vicinity. We paddled out for the rifle. They waited. We would have been torn to pieces had we landed. I shot the male. He dropped without a sound. The sight of the big male crumpling before their eyes drove the others into the mangroves, but when we landed they rushed out again and I shot one. It was the half-grown pup. The mother took shelter in the man-

The wild dogs of Albemarle Island

groves. I felt her vengeful eyes watching but could not see her. Then in a final deliberate hunt I went after the poor beast to finish the miserable job, leaving Florence in the canoe.

It was all so uncanny — stalking the now wary dog through the mangroves and among jagged lava ridges, being stalked by the animal at the same time. We hunted each other until I finally resorted to strategy, concealing myself among some high boulders. Soon the powerful tan head and shoulders appeared over a nearby ridge, a shot from the 30·30 and it was over. We felt so depressed that we had no appetite for work. When I was quite young I used to yearn for a gun. Then one day I found myself in Nova Scotia standing beside a magnificent bull moose who lifted his large reproachful eyes for a moment before he died. My desire for killing died then and there, I only do so now for food. This unsavoury day's work of mine with the dogs brought home to me again the repugnance of taking life unnecessarily, and I could only regret the capture of the pup that instigated the whole affair.

These islands have been the scene of so much killing that we were almost religious in our policy of taking no life. The impoverishment of the invaluable and irreplaceable wild life of the Galapagos, first by the buccaneers and whalers who knew no better,[1] and more recently by

[1] 'The Spaniards, when they first discover'd these Islands, found Multitudes of Guanos (iguanas), and Land-turtle or Tortoise, and named them the Gallapagos Islands. I do believe there is no place in the World that is so plentifully stored with those Animals. The Guanos here are fat and large as any that I ever saw;

yachtsmen and selfish scientists who should have known better, is a sad record. Here was a unique group, a well-equipped laboratory where Nature, the scientist, had performed the most perfect experiment on the differentiation of species existing to-day. It was this group that was largely responsible for one of the most sweeping revolutions of thought of modern times, for it was here that Charles Darwin, visiting the islands in the *Beagle*, first regimented his theories which were to influence coming generations so strongly.[1] And this group, so rich in scientific study, has been so thoroughly raped and robbed that on many of the islands whole species that flourished abundantly not long ago are now extinct or nearly so. The wholesale slaughter, for instance, of the most famous of Galapagos inhabitants, the giant land tortoise which originally populated the islands in incredible numbers,[2] is only to be compared with such other major examples of man's lack of foresight as the near-extermination of the bison, or that of the seal, now saved from extinction at the last minute by rigid policing by the National Authorities.

[1] *A Naturalist's Voyage*, London, 1845, by Charles Darwin.
[2] Dr. Townsend, Director of the New York Aquarium, who has made a thorough study of the Galapagos tortoise, believes that no less than ten million tortoises have been taken from the islands.

they are so tame that a Man may knock down twenty in an Hour's Time with a Club. The Land-turtle are here so numerous that 500 or 600 Men might subsist on them alone for several Months, without any other sort of Provisions: They are extraordinary large and fat; and so sweet, that no Pullet eats more pleasantly. ... There are great plenty of Turtle-Doves, so tame, that a Man may kill 5 or 6 dozen in a Forenoon with a stick. They are somewhat less than a Pigeon, and are very good Meat and commonly fat ...' – William Dampier, *A New Voyage Round the World*.

There have lately been rumours of the United States co-operating with Ecuador in protecting the remaining wild life of the Galapagos. To accomplish this the lid must be clamped down and it must become a criminal offence to kill or take away specimens of Galapagos life. The islands have already been closed theoretically by Ecuadorean law, but the only way to do this successfully is to police them, for owing to their isolation and uninhabited state unscrupulous visitors would continue to kill and take surreptitiously. It is too easy to go there without a clearance for the islands, stay as long as one likes, and sail away without having seen or been seen by humans. Policing them could easily be done by a pair of well-powered cruising vessels of coast-guard type, stationed permanently in the islands, patrolling their shores. Ecuador is probably unable to do this, but there is no reason why interested Americans cannot accomplish something along these lines through Ecuadorean co-operation. It is both a financial and a diplomatic problem, but one that should not be too difficult to solve. A movement toward this end is already under way I believe. I hope that something will come of it.

CHAPTER XXI

TAGUS COVE

ONE day — about a month after our last visit to Tagus Cove — we thought it was time to go to the Post Office. We started early and sailed down the coast. It did us good to get off for a bird's-eye view of the great island, the intimate details of which we had come to know so thoroughly from our work ashore. It helped readjust our point of view and develop a fuller perception of the land. It shrank our little world back to its proper scale as we drew away and watched it dwindle into nothingness at the foot of the greater cinder and lava mountain behind, where ominous pillars of steam rose constantly from the live craters on the upper northern slope. The magnitude and desolation of Albemarle came to us with more force now as the whole sweeping vista spread before us. To the south of Elizabeth Bay lay a great region of utter destruction, black and lifeless. Then from the bay half-way to Tagus Cove a thin sprinkling of plant life gave a deceptive green appearance. It looked almost fertile from a mile or so at sea. To the north again, was more bare lava country behind a wide sweeping bay.

Approaching Tagus Cove, we could see countless lava flows, curving wide black swathes through the thin green of the slopes. The shore became a low black plateau of gigantic clinkers and cinders. Across the strait lay Narborough — a single monstrous mountain of volcanic offal, protected and held close within the swelling breasts of Albemarle by the arms of its extended curving capes. Between, as a cushion, lay the narrow swift-flowing strait, teeming with fish. Tagus Cove was easily distinguished, for it lay exactly opposite the nearest part of Narborough, surrounded by a cluster of high ridge-like hills that marked it for what it was: an old flooded crater with the west side missing. Narborough protects it from the swell and makes it an ideal harbour. All around the inner cliffs of the cove are painted the names of the yachts and fishing vessels which have come there. The one I like best is the LOS ANGELES — CITY LIMITS sign, uprooted from its original location and transplanted here in Tagus Cove. For the American tuna boats that come all the way from California to fish Galapagos waters this is no idle jest.

We anchored in our usual place — steering straight in for the SIERRA sign until abreast the NOURMAHAL where we dropped the anchor in about eight fathoms. A little later we were heavy-hearted. Our mail box was empty. It is not so bad if you miss a mail at home. But when your round trip time to the post office is two days and a night, that is something else.

We stayed two days trying to discover a tuna boat, to send a wireless. Just as we had given up and were starting home, we saw masts and rigging over a point on Narborough. Joyfully we headed there. In a little while we could be in touch for a bit with the outside world. We came close. We tidied up a bit below — the captain would probably come aboard. Perhaps he would like some of that marvellous Chilean brandy. . . . I turned to slow the engine. A burst of Diesel smoke spouted from the other boat, and she forged rapidly away toward the open sea. Downcast, we rolled there close to Narborough, not understanding. Then we started home. A mile beyond, to our great amazement, we rounded a point and saw a second tuna boat. Well — this was luck! Let the other unfriendly idiots avoid us if they pleased. . . . We were within a hundred yards, almost alongside, when the scene was repeated. The powerful low-hung vessel slipped away under our very noses, leaving only a smell of fish blended with Diesel smoke. In a few moments she was out of sight. Did they think we were lepers? Had our appearance in our isolation become so terrifying that even fishermen fled? Suddenly I saw light. They were poaching unlicensed in Galapagos waters. They thought we were Ecuadorean officials — hence the quick getaway. The Galapagos solitude closed down upon us and we steered a lonely course back to our more friendly camp, thirty miles away.

CHAPTER XXII

LIFE AT PELICAN LAGOON

ON April 23rd when I awoke and dived overboard
for my morning plunge, I was shocked by the cold of the
water — a delicious unexpected chill. I measured the
temperature and it was 68 instead of the usual 76 or 78.
The constantly changing eddies of the Humboldt Current
cause this variation. It is sometimes as low as 60 on one
side of Albemarle and 80 on the other. This accounts for
the remarkable variation in flora and fauna. Two days
later the water in our bay was nearly 80 again. We found
the currents constantly changing in this manner, bringing
with them varying forms of sea life.

In contrast to the currents, however, our weather was fairly uniform. The land breeze (the east wind) would blow fresh from mid-morning till early afternoon, when it weakened and finally swung through north into the west and blew strongly until sunset, making our bay quite rough. During these afternoon hours the *Svaap* pitched and jerked at her chains, and we were glad to have our two anchors out.

We timed our daily routine to coincide with the winds. By starting early we could get in during the morning calm. This was a pleasant half-mile paddle before the steady east wind began to blow, but it became a hard task if we slept too long. In place of an alarm clock we had a school of sea lions who came each morning to wake us with their bellowing — frolicking around the *Svaap* until we were ready to leave. Then they accompanied us on our trip ashore. We had other regular visitors every morning. A giant ray liked to cruise near by, a huge sea turtle would blow close alongside. Schools of fish were feeding in a dozen places in the bay, each with its hosts of birds overhead diving for the small fry that were forced to the surface. A pair of little penguins came each morning too — to dart around like tiny comets, snooping inquisitively all the while.

When lunch time came, after a morning's work ashore, we would hoist our sail on the outrigger and go racing out before the wind, tearing along like the famed flying outriggers of Raiatea in the South Seas. Then, after a leisurely lunch and a siesta, we were ready to return to work when the west wind came rollicking in from the sea. Thus we sailed back and forth, feeling like three buccaneers of old, putting the daily winds to work and changing what might have been a trying ordeal into a gay adventure.

Once or twice a day, when we became too fatigued with our work and needed relaxation, we would swim in our own lagoon. A smooth flow of lava ran down into our pool on one side and made an excellent runway. Beyond were patches of brilliant yellow sand with curious volcanic formations here and there. Rainbow-hued fish darted in and out of little underwater caves and grottos.

As soon as we threw off our clothes and plunged in, the sea lions would come to play, darting around and under us with great enthusiasm. The pelican would dive from his perch now and then when we started up a school of small fish. Our little pair of penguins would join us, and perhaps a big marine iguana would be swimming there too. The peefer bird preferred to sit disconsolately on the gunwale of the canoe. I would take a long dive under water, open my eyes, and find one of our penguins with his head stretched forward, examining me intently. Then we would both come up for air, each thinking what an odd looking fellow the other was. Those days I shall always remember as among the happiest of my life. It was all a great adventure — a strange Eden-life of which we shall have long-enduring memories.

We would work late ashore, until the sun had set and our man-o'-war bird had come to roost for the night in his accustomed place. Dusk, and the evening calm would fall upon the world. We had that feeling of infinite satisfaction that comes only from a hard day's work well done. There was a moon now; at night it was lovely, with our cloud-wrapped volcanic peaks towering on three sides. The cooling mountains sent down a gentle whispering night breeze. Before it, we would sail out to sea in our primitive canoe, casting weird reflections on the shimmering bay. On evenings like this, after a day of the hardest labour ashore in the blazing sun, we would wish the *Svaap* were miles away, so that to reach her we could sail on and on over our restful sea.

Dan would prepare dinner while Florence straightened up the cabin and I worked on my daily notes. Sooky the bear would bounce all over everything. Afterwards a quiet talk on deck, sipping our evening drink, a long refreshing rum and lime. On shore in the evening a few mosquitoes appeared. On board we had none. The stars slid overhead. The sea lions came to make their evening call. The moon shone with a glorious soft radiance on the usually grim lava beds ashore, and on our strange little Iguana Tree Island, and on the brooding mountains. It would be cool now, although we were almost under the very line of the equator itself, and we would lie down to sleep, tired but at peace with our world.

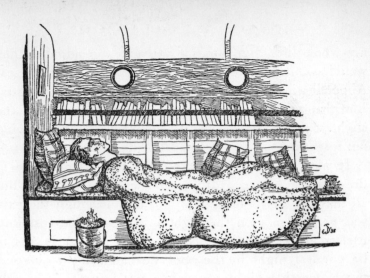

CHAPTER XXIII

BUT IF YOU GOT APPENDICITIS

THEN suddenly — in the midst of our idyllic existence —
I awoke one morning before the dawn after an endless
succession of strange foreboding dreams, my whole
abdomen racked by intense pain. My first thought was
ptomaine poisoning. We treated it accordingly. I tried
not to worry — everything would be all right. I had the
constitution of a horse.

I found myself doubled up with pain, sitting in the
companion-way staring out to sea. A horrible dread was
creeping over me . . . people had always asked me what
do you do if you get sick — and my answer had always
been you don't get sick. I never had been really sick in

231

my whole life. But what if you got appendicitis, they would ask. . . . Appendicitis. . . . I stared out at the sea. Appendicitis! What *would* I do if I got appendicitis? But that was impossible — I had never had even the slightest sign of it. Forget it! I told myself. But I could not forget it.

It was Sunday, May 20th. We sent Dan ashore to draw, while Florence did what she could for me. But all that day devils tore at my insides, although the pain was general, not on the right side where that insidious useless little organ lay. Night closed down. It was to be our last night in the spot we had come to love so much, for that night the pain crept remorselessly over to the right side, down below the ribs, and concentrated there. There was no further doubt. I had forgotten our evil genius. But now I thought I heard him chuckling diabolically. His hour had come at last.

We held a very serious consultation that night — towards midnight, Florence, Dan, and I. What to do? If we started for Guayaquil, the nearest place with surgeons, it meant bucking the current and winds for more than six hundred miles — perhaps two weeks. Panama was a thousand miles, with a more favourable current, but doldrums and squalls: ten days at the least if we were lucky and had enough petrol to help us through the calm regions. But the other two — Florence and Dan — could they navigate accurately enough to *find* Panama? I was beyond helping them.

Oh — we were in a fine fix out there at the end of the

earth. We decided to make an effort to find a tuna boat before doing anything else. We could get medical advice by wireless through them. If they evaded us as they had done before, even supposing we were lucky enough to locate one . . . we tried not to think of that.

Florence was now in command of the *Svaap*. At dawn, Monday, May 21st, she and Dan began a heroic struggle with our two heavy anchors and their sixty fathoms of chain. We weren't any too sure they could get them up — for my strength had always heretofore done the major heavy work. For two hours they worked, foot by foot, until at last the anchors were up. Florence steered for Narborough where she knew by experience she would find a boat if there was one in the vicinity. The chance was remote — for they only come at intervals and then only for a day or so to get bait before going out to sea again. One might sometimes look for months and find no boat.

'We see a boat!' It was on the Narborough shore, they told me.

The clock at the front of my berth had crept slowly around and around and it was late afternoon now. We had hunted all the shores where the boats were apt to be, and she was on the last stretch. She was obviously the only boat — our one chance of help. We grew tense, wondering if she would run as the others had. The drama was more than I could bear. I dragged myself to the companion-way and hung there with my head outside to watch. We came close. I saw men in the surf seining. They paid no attention to us. It was the *Santa Cruz*, the boat we had met in Tagus Cove on our first trip there. We had won the first point. I crawled back to my bunk and collapsed.

From then on I have a strange jumble of vague haunting memories that refuse to congeal into clarity — and a few vivid mind pictures etched indelibly in my brain. There was the wireless that came from a naval hospital in California in reply to Florence's frantic broadcast over the *Santa Cruz's* radio for medical instructions:

ALLOW PATIENT NO FOOD OR DRINK KEEP AFFECTED PARTS PACKED IN ICE MOVE PATIENT AT ONCE TO HOSPITAL

We were lucky in having the ice — for the *Santa Cruz* had tons of it, to keep her glistening tuna on their long voyage to San Pedro. I came to sympathize with those tuna. My whole mid-section was at once packed and frozen numb and remained that way from then on. But 'Move patient at once to hospital!' The irony of it! Instead we moved to Tagus Cove and anchored. The *Santa Cruz* followed to stand by and await developments. We all still hoped the thing would abate, especially now that it was under ice.

Night fell, and constantly increasing pain. It was obvious that the emergency was real. Captain Hage of the *Santa Cruz* knew of a case where the Navy had come to the aid of a stricken sailor on a fishing boat off the Californian coast. This gave Florence a single straw to which she clung — and the rest of us too — and with Ward King, the wireless operator, she sat beside the instrument for hours that night trying to get a message through to Admiral Crosley in Balboa, asking if some naval vessel near by could come to our aid. Meanwhile Dan worked sleeplessly with ice compresses.

We were buoyed up by hope — but the hours dragged on and the wireless dead spot between Tagus Cove and Panama barred us off like a wall. At last Chatham, Massachusetts, picked up the appeal, relayed it back down to Panama, and at midnight came word from the admiral:

REGRET NO SHIPS IN VICINITY

It was obvious that things were in the last extreme. I had not known it was possible to suffer so and retain full consciousness and mental control. The last had become a definite struggle — I clung deliberately to sanity as a man fallen overboard at night from a fast sailing ship would cling to a line, feeling it slip slowly through his grip, inch by inch, wondering when the end of the line would come. My line slipped a little now and then, and I would have fleeting moments of delirium like the terror-stricken nightmares of childhood. Then my grip would tighten again and the line would slip no more for the time being.

The two in the cramped wireless room tried other channels without hope. The key chattered away for hours sending its messages on unseen wings through the air.

The miracle of wireless! Unseen wings through the air with the speed of light! Wings! . . . Planes! . . .

Sometime in the early morning hours the worried admiral received another message signed Florence Robinson:

SITUATION DESPERATE COULD PLANE WITH SURGEON REACH GALAPAGOS

. . . and at sunrise next day, Tuesday, the reply came clicking over the instrument to bring at last a ray of hope to the tired girl:

REQUESTING AUTHORITY FROM WASHINGTON TO SEND PLANES TO GALAPAGOS

That was the beginning of the second phase of our ordeal — the phase of hope. The first had been one of black futility. Monday had been a year. Monday night . . . weeks and months of endless icy compresses, slow torture, and strange mental gyrations — until it was Tuesday and a third year had begun. Time was growing short. Anton Hage would tell me there was still a swollen lump there, when the ice was being changed, and as long as there was a lump the appendix hadn't broken. He knew, for he had had the same thing. An appendix *couldn't* rupture right away. Of course not. I was good for several days yet. There *must* be a lump. Of *course* there was a lump I would say . . . but I couldn't feel any, and all the while I knew it had burst already sometime Monday night. Peritonitis had set in.

I became obsessed with the idea that I must not let

myself slip into delirium or fall asleep, for you see, so long as I could stay conscious I could not die. So day and night I had constant changes of cold compresses on my head, with more of the ice that belonged rightfully to those poor tuna alongside. And I constantly mocked that gnawing thirst that had developed, by rinsing my mouth with ice water but never swallowing a drop, for that would have lessened my chances. It kept us all occupied, which was better than just waiting. Anton Hage and Dan alternated at the work whenever Florence left to stand by the wireless.

The wireless had become the focal point of our very existence. And at noon on Tuesday the instrument spelled out the message that lifted the edge of the curtain of hopelessness that had been closing down around us. Florence came hurrying over from the *Santa Cruz* with shining eyes and I knew the message before she said a word. It was a radio from Admiral Crosley:

DESTROYER AND PLANES WITH SURGEONS LEAVING FOR GALAPAGOS AS SOON AS POSSIBLE

After that I remember very little except the ceaseless ministrations and encouragements of Florence, Dan, and Anton Hage. The men on the *Santa Cruz* crept in one by one and tried eagerly to help in some way or to bring cheer. These rough fishermen had taken Florence and Dan under their wing and mothered them. Already crowded on their small craft they had made a place for them, and fed them. Under their long neglected beards were the men — the real men that are bred by lifelong toil on the sea. I have no words of praise high enough for these men of the *Santa Cruz*, and in particular for Ward King who stood by his wireless almost constantly three days and nights, and for her master Anton Hage.

The story of those days is graphically told by a few terse messages received at home by my mother. The radio companies, the Press, and the Navy, knowing her agony of worry, took it upon their shoulders to relay to her each bulletin they received. For days she sat by her telephone waiting for news. The only direct reports that she had, excluding newspaper stories and radio broadcasts which were largely based on rumour, were the following:

CHICAGO ILLINOIS   1934 MAY 22 AM 8:53
RADIO CAME LAST NIGHT STATING FLORENCE HAS ACUTE APPENDICITIS BUT NOW FIND IT IS ROBBIE INSTEAD HOPE FOR REASSURING NEWS WILL KEEP YOU INFORMED FLORENCE HAS RADIOED APPEAL TO NAVY TO SEND PLANES WITH MEDICAL AID

MACKAY RADIO COMPANY   1934 MAY 22 PM 8:00
WILL HAVE DIRECT CONTACT WITH MOTOR TRAWLER SANTA CRUZ DURING THIS EVENING SANTA CRUZ IS STANDING BY SVAAP IN TAGUS COVE ALBEMARLE ISLAND GALAPAGOS

NAVAL RADIO BALBAO CZ   1934 MAY 22
DESTROYER AND PLANES WITH SURGEONS LEAVING FOR GALAPAGOS AS SOON AS POSSIBLE

                                        W S CROSLEY BALBOA

MACKAY RADIO COMPANY   1934 MAY 22 PM 10:50
INTERCEPTED MESSAGE FROM SANTA CRUZ TO ADMIRAL
CROSLEY AT BALBOA READING RUSH PLANES EARLIEST POSSI-
BLE MOMENT EVERY MOMENT COUNTS APPRECIATE CO-
OPERATION GREATLY   FLORENCE C ROBINSON

MACKAY RADIO COMPANY   1934 MAY 22 PM 11:00
TANKER CATHWOOD NOW ABOUT FIFTY MILES FROM CANAL
REPORT THEY HAVE CONTACTED NAVY RADIO CANAL ZONE
STATE TWO PLANES SCHEDULED TO LEAVE COCO SOLO AIR
BASE FIVE A.M. TO-MORROW MORNING FOR YACHT SVAAP

MACKAY RADIO COMPANY   1934 MAY 23 AM 12:20
RADIO OPERATOR ON SANTA CRUZ REPORTS PATIENT
COMING ALONG WELL BUT HAD SINKING SPELL ABOUT
MIDNIGHT WILL KEEP YOU INFORMED

MACKAY RADIO COMPANY   1934 MAY 23 AM 2:45
SANTA CRUZ OPERATOR REPORTS PATIENT SEEMS TO BE
GETTING WEAKER NOW DOES NOT MOVE ANY MORE CAN
ONLY WHISPER VERY WEAKLY

MACKAY RADIO COMPANY   1934 MAY 23 AM 7:00
TANKER FIFTY MILES OFF BALBOA REPORTS SIGHTING TWO
PLANES AT THAT POINT PLANES LEFT FROM COCO SOLO
ATLANTIC SIDE FLYING OVER ISTHMUS AND NOT STARTING
FROM BALBOA AS EXPECTED

MACKAY RADIO COMPANY   1934 MAY 23 AM 8:00
SANTA CRUZ REPORTS PATIENT SUFFERING CONSIDERABLY
BUT CONDITION BETTER THAN AT MIDNIGHT PLANES DUE
TO ARRIVE THREE FIFTEEN P.M.

NAVY DEPARTMENT WASHINGTON   1934 MAY 23
NO INFORMATION AS TO ARRIVAL OF PLANES OR CONDITION
OF YOUR SON PERIOD WILL KEEP YOU INFORMED THROUGH
COMMANDANT FIRST NAVAL DISTRICT BOSTON MASS

                            CHIEF OF NAVAL OPERATIONS

NAVY YARD BOSTON   1934 MAY 23 AM
FOLLOWING RECEIVED COMMA SANTA CRUZ REPORTS PATIENT
CONDITION AT THREE PM SAME AS LAST NIGHT VERY WEAK
SUFFERING OCCASIONAL VIOLENT PAINS IN ABDOMEN

On board the *Svaap* our little drama dragged on
interminably. Late on Tuesday we learned that the planes
would start at daylight next morning. Dawn of Wednesday came. The planes would be preparing for the take
off. I had flown from the Coco Solo base myself and
could visualize the scene there. Engines roaring.
Flashes of flames from exhausts throwing dim hurrying
figures into momentary relief. The noisy excitement as
the planes go down the runways into the water. There
would probably be false starts in the mushy calm air
of a drizzly Panamanian morning in the rainy season.
Assuming the planes did get off, overloaded with surgeons, supplies, and fuel, there would be a thousand
miles to fly over the Pacific in a region I knew well —
with vicious rains and line squalls the first half of the
way, and head winds the last half. Just a routine flight
for the Navy men, with no thought of reward or fame.
But the first time in history that planes had flown to
Galapagos.

As the day wore away and sunset came with no word from the planes, the false strength I had drawn from anticipation oozed away. I had been fighting mightily to live — but now suddenly I did not care what happened. If I died it would not matter much — but what if on account of me those men in the planes were lost? Soon it would be dark. If they had not come by then they were lost. There are no landing-places in mid-Pacific.

The *Santa Cruz* had steamed out into the Strait to make a conspicuous mark to help the planes find the Cove. Soon she would return. Someone lit our gimbal lamp in the cabin, and nearly set the *Svaap* on fire, starting nervously as a siren blared loudly in the strait. It was the *Santa Cruz*. She had sighted the planes. Five minutes later two naval surgeons were in the tiny cabin of *Svaap*. . . .

They set to work at once.

CHAPTER XXIV

THE PLANES CAME AT DUSK

THE planes came at dusk — the dusk of day and the dusk of life. But with their arrival the will to live returned with a rush.

At home, mother's bulletins continued:

MACKAY RADIO COMPANY   1934 MAY 23
MOTOR TRAWLER SHASTA NORTH OF GALAPAGOS REPORTS
PLANES DUE ANY TIME NOW WITH ONE HUNDRED EIGHTY
MILES TO GO WORD RECEIVED FROM SANTA CRUZ VIA NAVY
RADIO BALBOA THAT ROBINSONS CONDITION VERY CRITICAL
AND AT TIMES VERY WEAK BUT HOLDING HIS OWN

242

THE PLANES CAME AT DUSK

NAVY YARD BOSTON   1934 MAY 23 PM 10:30
FOLLOWING RECEIVED FROM GALAPAGOS QUOTE PLANE
DETACHMENT ARRIVED TAGUS COVE SIX FORTY PM MEDI-
CAL OFFICERS EXAMINED PATIENT AND REPORT CONDITION
CRITICAL PROBABLY RUPTURED APPENDIX WITH GENERAL
PERITONITIS IMMEDIATE OPERATION NOT ADVISABLE DUE
TO PATIENTS GENERAL CONDITION PERIOD UPON ARRIVAL
DESTROYER HALE WILL TRANSFER PATIENT WITH MEDICAL
OFFICERS TO THAT VESSEL AND SEND TO BALBOA AFTER
PLANES ARE SERVICED MRS ROBINSON WILL RETURN IN HALE
UNQUOTE

NAVY YARD BOSTON   1934 MAY 24 PM 4:15
FOLLOWING RECEIVED QUOTE AT FOUR FIFTEEN PM CON-
DITION MR ROBINSON CRITICAL USING ALL MEANS AVAIL-
ABLE TO INCREASE HIS STRENGTH NOW EXPECT OPERATE
IMMEDIATELY UPON ARRIVAL HALE PERIOD HALE DUE TO
ARRIVE TAGUS COVE SEVEN PM TODAY THURSDAY

MACKAY RADIO COMPANY   1934 MAY 24
LATEST BULLETIN PATIENT IMPROVING INFLAMMATION
LOCALIZED SURGEONS ENCOURAGED DESTROYER HALE DUE
GALAPAGOS THIS EVENING WILL START RETURN IN THREE
HOURS

NAVY YARD BOSTON   1934 MAY 24
ROBBIE STRICKEN WITH APPENDICITIS SUNDAY TWO PLANES
AND DESTROYER WITH SURGEONS ARRIVED FROM BALBOA
IS IN GOOD CONDITION AND RESTING COMFORTABLY NO
OPERATION YET TILL FURTHER DEVELOPMENTS WILL PROBA-

BLY GO TO PANAMA ON DESTROYER WILL KEEP YOU IN-
FORMED MUCH LOVE

FLORENCE[1]

MACKAY RADIO COMPANY   1934 MAY 24 PM 10:19
DESTROYER HALE JUST ARRIVED TAGUS COVE AND SURGEON
NOW OPERATING

The planes came Wednesday. From then until the
Hale arrived Thursday evening there were hypodermics,
and intravenous glucose-saline solution to build up
strength. We had scarcely stopped rolling from the
displacement wave of the *Hale* before a loaded stretcher
was being handed to a big navy launch from the *Svaap* and
we were transferred to the destroyer. I had seen nothing
but the top of my berth for five days. Now I had a momentary glimpse of outside once more — just a ten-second
flash of the amazingly crowded Tagus Cove, and Narborough across the way, all softened from its usual
grimness by a supremely beautiful halo of lingering sunset colours. I soaked up every detail of it like a photographic film, wanting to keep it to take with me. Then
I was in the captain's berth. They were going to operate
at once. We had a few minutes together, Florence and I.
It was time for our evening rum punch. Florence produced it somehow against all naval rules . . . and sat
with me. The thought was in both our minds that perhaps

[1] This was the first direct news from us. We had not realized that the world
would be following every step in our isolated drama. We did not want to worry
the family until there was some hope to offer too. Florence waited until medical
help had come before sending the message.

it was the last one we should have together. She drank hers. I could only put my lips to mine, but I drank in her beauty, and swelled with pride in this girl who could endure such anguish and still smile. The door opened. They were ready to operate.

I had time for one more vivid picture — the operating-room — just the sort of place I who love the sea would have chosen. Just the place for a sailor to take the big gamble. The officers' wardroom. I was on their dining-table. Flood lights hung overhead. The two naval surgeons standing ready. Over the ether mask I could see a pair of big shining brass portholes, and navigation instruments on the walls. I felt at home. I relaxed and breathed deeply. Florence was waiting outside . . . Florence . . . Florence . . . Just a little while. . . .

It was morning again. Outside my porthole flying fish darted from the tops of waves. A sapphire sea slid by with unaccountable swiftness. Then I remembered — I was no longer on *Svaap*, she was deserted back there in Tagus Cove, dismantled for the time being. . . . The destroyer trembled with speed.

Another morning two days later. Palm trees and green grass outside my porthole. The destroyer was quiet now. Gorgas Hospital. A comfortable bed. Florence looking less worn and haggard. Everything was going to be all right now. I sank into a deep sleep.

CHAPTER XXV

A DEBT I OWE

WHEN the debt you owe is that of your life itself, it becomes futile to write of appreciation, gratitude, and everlasting remembrance. The words become hollow empty shells, failing utterly. The men of the *Santa Cruz*, for instance, what can I say to them? Or the Navy men — Admiral Crosley in Balboa and the officers of the General Board in Washington who forgot about red tape and acted before it was too late. Or Commander Molten who organized and led the flight to Galapagos. Or officers Halland and Kane who brought their planes a thousand miles over unflown seas through endless tropical rains and squalls. Or the naval surgeons Hutchinson and Yarbrough who did exactly the right thing at the right moment. Or Lieutenant-Commander

Browne of the *Hale*, quiet and reassuring through the turmoil of that frantic mad night in Tagus. And then there were the other officers who took part, and the enlisted men. . . .

It is impossible to write of the part that each man played. There were so many, and all showed the same eager spirit. But to mention a single example is to describe the attitude of everyone concerned. William K. de Pue was the Pharmacist's Mate of the *Hale*. During the return trip to Balboa he took it upon himself to stand by practically twenty-four hours a day, giving Florence and Dan a chance to recover somewhat from their ordeal. His constant care contributed greatly to my increasing strength. He proved to be not only an excellent Pharmacist's Mate (a naval combination of medical assistant and nurse) but a good psychologist as well, when I tottered precariously on the edge of a strange mental abyss. Post-operation duties are not very pleasant — but this husky sailor performed them all gently and cheerfully, with as much consideration as one would receive in the finest hospital in the land. De Pue stands for just one line in the page of debt I owe — representative of all that were there in Tagus those fateful days. I can only say that I am proud of the privilege of knowing them all. If they read this account I hope they will find between the lines the things that are too deep to write.

The flight to Galapagos by the two naval planes was highly publicized at the time. The newspapers were

quick to see the drama of the 'mercy flight'. But I
wonder how many of those who read the story over their
morning coffee thought of the significance of the whole
thing — how it symbolized the new era in which we live,
tying together inseparably the two great new world
factors, wireless and flight, already so familiar as to be
taken almost for granted. But I still cannot take for
granted the fact that from a small fishing vessel in an
isolated Pacific archipelago it was possible to receive
over the air medical instructions from California; that
in our crisis we were able to appeal to the proper authorities in Panama and Washington via this same little
wireless outfit. Nor can I take it for granted that two
naval planes carrying fifteen men, including two surgeons and complete operating equipment, could leave
Coco Solo on the Atlantic side of the Canal in the morning, and be riding to anchor in Galapagos the same evening!
Two surgeons, called for an early breakfast in Coco Solo,
saving a life in Tagus Cove before dinner the same day!
It is all too fantastic to believe. As for it happening to
me — it must have been a troubled dream, long ago.

The day for excitement over long ocean flights is
past. But this naval flight to Galapagos is more signifi-
cant than most. Ocean flights are synonymous with
weeks and months of careful preparation. They entail
special equipment and special study of meteorological
and other conditions along the route. This was something far different. Admiral Crosley called the air base
on the morning of May 22nd, and asked if they could

make the flight. Commander Molten replied that he could do it if he could have a destroyer to refuel him in Galapagos for the return trip. At 10 a.m. he was informed that the destroyer was available and was instructed to go ahead. Twenty hours later, at dawn on the 23rd, the two planes left the runways for the thousand-mile flight over waters never before flown, in a region where the weather conditions were very poorly known. Not only that, but the planes themselves were just plain standard equipment, and they carried, amazingly enough, everything necessary for the treatment and operation of a critically ill man, supplies for the fifteen men, spare parts, and heaven knows what else. The whole thing went off with the smoothness of well-oiled machinery, speaking volumes for the stage aviation has reached, and for the perfection of naval organization.

Commander R. P. Molten, then in command of the air base, was kind enough to write for me the details of the flight, and a copy of his résumé of the trip written in an unofficial report to the Navy Department in Washington. I had written him asking for some of the details, thinking to reconstruct the flight in this book. But his matter-of-fact account and keen observation of the situation in Tagus Cove give the whole picture so vividly that I can do no better than reproduce his own words here:

At 5 A.M. May 22nd, I was called to the phone and Admiral Crosley said that you had acute appendicitis at Galapagos and what could we do. I told him that I had planes that could make the run out, but I would need petrol out there; also I was against having a desperately ill person too far from land in a plane — so recommended that he get hold of two destroyers, one to head for Tagus, the other to be in Balboa, to back us up. He said O.K. At 10 A.M. Washington told the Admiral to go ahead. He called in destroyers *Hale* and *Buchanan* and turned them over to me. While they were fueling I had the wrecking barge *Mary Anne* loaded: 1400 gallons petrol, oil, wing tip float, propeller, and a few engine spares. Sent her over to the fuel dock and put the gear on the *Hale*. She started through the Canal that afternoon and lit out for Galapagos. I issued orders to Patrol Squadron 5, Lieut. Comdr. Halland, to get two planes ready to leave at daybreak on the 23rd. These planes were 5P4 and 5P8, a patrol type built by Consolidated Aircraft Corp. of Buffalo, N.Y. They are monoplanes with a wing span of about 105 feet, powered with two-geared Wright cyclone engines of about 545 h.p. each. They carry 1240 gallons of petrol normally. Can carry about 1600. On this trip due to the doctors and extra gear, to say nothing of a large amount of canned food and water, we were heavily loaded. No special or outstanding preparations were made — just details and more details, and those little things which pop up.

The rainy season had settled down which meant no more steady trades, but rain, and calm at daylight with southerly winds later. We left the runways at 6 A.M. but it was as I feared: mushy air, a heavy load, and no wind. Lieut. Kane made 1st attempt but plane was too deep in water. He returned and cleaned a couple of plugs. By then a light air had sprung up so we taxied out to the breakwater and took off heading west. Were in the air at six-forty. After passing Balboa the wind increased steadily from SW. to force of 18 m.p.h. The trip out was reasonably rotten. Flew about 100 to 150 feet off the water all the way. Heavy tropical rains for over five hours straight. We arrived at Tagus Cove at 7 p.m. From then on you have the picture ... The trip back was uneventful except a fair amount of thick weather with Line Squalls as we approached Panama. We arrived back at Coco Solo at 5.15 p.m. on the 25th.

There is no question there are high spots ... vivid, never-forgettable pictures that stand out from the drab background of routine. As we approached where *we hoped* to find Galapagos night was closing in. We were at sea and had none too much petrol. We had to find land before dark. You know Galapagos is not like a populated island. We knew there would be no lights or towns. It was not only a comforting sight, but one of beauty, when we saw the peaks of the Galapagos rise majestically out of the sea, backed by a sky of indescribable beauty. The islands themselves are very forbidding from the air. They seem to repel intrusion.

THE FIFTEEN MEN WHO FLEW TO TAGUS COVE, GALAPAGOS

Commander R. P. Molten
Lieutenant-Commander H. E. Halland
Lieutenant-Commander G. L. Compo
Lieutenant J. L. Kane
Boatswain P. J. Byrne
Lieutenant-Commander R. W. Hutchinson
  (Medical Corps)
Lieutenant C. D. Yarbrough (Medical Corps)

Chief Machinist's Mate C. P. Benedict
Machinist Mate F. H. Cederberg
Machinist Mate R. L. Wilson
Machinist Mate E. J. Getzy
Machinist J. P. Ittner
Radioman F. J. Uhl
Radioman J. A. Spraggins
Pharmacist's Mate J. R. Sumpter

THE CREW OF THE 'SANTA CRUZ'

Anton Hage	Master
Ward King	Radioman
Mark Temple	Engineer
Ted Johnston	Cook
Peder Sigvard Bjerkevaag	Seaman
James J. Moore	Seaman
James J. Moore, Jr.	Seaman
Gust Olsen	Seaman
Joe de Reis	Seaman
Anton Rodin	Seaman
Murray Ross	Seaman
Paul Torlen	Seaman

The *Santa Cruz*, owned in San Diego by Lewis, Simas, Jones, was worked by the crew as a co-operative venture, on shares, so that the delay in standing by the *Svaap* affected every man. The men of the *Santa Cruz* were born in half a dozen countries. They have adopted the United States as their native land, and the sea for their living. To the last man they upheld the traditions of their profession.

CHAPTER XXVI

LET ME TELL YOU ABOUT *MY* OPERATION

I HAVE learned to my amazement that practically everyone alive has had acute appendicitis. A flood of letters came in for some months afterwards, telling of the extraordinary circumstances of *their* operation. The depressing accounts of most amazing after effects, suffered it seems for years afterwards, did much to cheer my weeks in the Gorgas Hospital in Balboa. There were letters from people whose appendix had ruptured in mid-ocean, on mountain tops, in the desert, in the jungles of Siam. I have heard from people whose crisis had occurred during almost every occupation except flagpole sitting and marathon dancing, which is rather surprising, for one would expect these occupations to produce an abnormal number of cases.

Just in case there are any left who might be interested in learning about *my* operation — someone perhaps just about to swim the Atlantic, worried about his appendix — here's the details.

Seriously, the appendix is an important consideration to anyone who is going to be out of touch with surgical facilities for any length of time. For some inexplicable reason it seems to prefer to flare up in the most awkward places. I know of cases which caused any amount of trouble and expense just because they occurred at the wrong time. And also some which proved fatal for the same reason. The modern appendix operation is such a minor affair that I really think that it is advisable for anyone who plans to be out of touch with civilization for any length of time to have the thing taken out before leaving, just as a precautionary measure. It seems to be the common belief that you always have one or more warning attacks before anything serious happens. This is not true. I had never in my life had anything the matter with my appendix, or anything else inside me, until it flared up that morning off Pelican Lagoon, a thousand miles from anywhere. That was May 20th. It was sometime during Monday night, May 21st, that the pains reached their climax, which no doubt was when the appendix burst. So it was only thirty-six hours from the very first warning until the beginning of what would have been the end had not help arrived. When the Naval surgeons operated on the night óf May 24th peritonitis was so far advanced that the pus welled out through the incision in such quantities that they could only put in a drain tube. So the margin between a first attack and the end may be as little as two or three days. My constitution, which has always been perfect, was the only thing which tipped the scales and allowed the miracle of my recovery. I bring out this point to emphasize my admonition: If you are going to go to an isolated part of the world, consider well the advisability of having your appendix out first. We, with our experience fresh in mind, believe so strongly in this caution, that my wife, Florence, just previous to our recent departure for the South Pacific again, walked into the hospital at home and had her perfectly healthy appendix removed.

To conclude the account of *my* operation, I fortunately fell into the care of Dr. Troy W. Earhart of the Gorgas Hospital, one of the world's great surgeons. He made a second drain incision for a secondary infection which developed in my side. Then for weeks I had two miniature oil wells flowing from within me. Two months later, when the poison was all out and the incisions had closed, Dr. Earhart operated again to clean up the remaining shreds of the appendix and straighten things up generally. Ten days later we boarded a freighter and sailed for home to recuperate. And that is the story of *my* operation.

Since this book is apt to be read by the kind of people who go to far places, or hope to, and since the reader will probably *not* take my advice and have his appendix out first, here is what to do if you should be so unfortunate as to wake up some morning with a violent pain in your right side:

(1) Go to bed and stay there flat on your back and don't move.

(2) Don't eat or drink a single thing. A laxative is the worst possible thing. The idea is to let your organs lie as quietly as possible. If they are put in motion through bodily movement or through the process of digestion, they tend to irritate the inflamed appendix if it has not burst, or to spread the infection if it has burst.

(3) Keep the painful area constantly packed with ice if you can get it. Improvise an ice-bag if you have none.

(4) Get a surgeon brought to you with the utmost possible rapidity if that is possible, or yourself brought to a place where medical attention may be had.

You won't mind the hunger much, but the thirst will be bad after the first couple of days. You will lose a terrifying amount of weight (I lost thirty-five pounds in a few days). But when the doctors do get at you they can quickly make up for the loss of body moisture by intramuscular injections of saline solution; and you will have a fair chance to come through.

CHAPTER XXVII

SVAAP NEARS THE END

THOSE who have followed the adventurous career of
Svaap will wonder what happened to her. I am afraid
that this time there is no happy ending. Instead of an
honoured peaceful haven in which to end her days,
the brave little ketch has become an unhappy pawn of the
Fate that pursued her last voyage. It was realized, on
that final blurred night in Tagus, that I would be out of
commission for a long time if I recovered at all. And
so the captain of the *Hale* gave Florence and Dan men
to help strip the yacht of everything valuable. There

was no alternative but to desert her there for the time being. So when the planes had gone, and the *Hale* steamed north with the three of us aboard, and the *Santa Cruz* put to sea again — poor *Svaap* was left: a dismantled hull riding to its two anchors, alone down there in Tagus Cove.

Two months later, still in Balboa growing stronger all the time, I began to make plans again. President Roosevelt passed through the canal bound for Hawaii, and we had the pleasure of thanking him for what the Navy had done. With his famous warmth of personality he actually left us with the feeling that it had been a good thing for the Navy to have had the opportunity to make the flight. But even so I still felt very guilty about all the commotion I had caused, and wanted to do something to show my gratitude. Suddenly it occurred to me that it would be a fine thing to give the *Svaap* to the Naval Academy at Annapolis. The greatest thing you can give is the thing you love the most. Accordingly, the Academy was notified of the gift, and a short note to the President explained my desire. I started preparations to have the *Svaap* brought back to Panama to be put in condition to be sent to Annapolis. Just when things were all set, and the salvage party was ready to leave Panama for Galapagos, we learned from Washington that the Naval Academy would be unable to accept the gift due to legal complications. This was a bitter blow. I cancelled the contract to have *Svaap* brought back to Panama. For the time being she would be all right in Tagus Cove. Before long I would be able to go for her myself. At this time *Svaap* was in very good condition, perfectly safe there where she lay.

Several months elapsed. One day there came a letter from the President, in answer to mine informing him of the gift of *Svaap*. The letter had been mislaid by some secretary going on leave and had not come to light until the end of September. The President had heard nothing of the matter. He regretted that the gift had been declined and hoped that the offer was still open, being 'entirely in agreement with you that the *Svaap* would be of great value to the Navy at Annapolis in stimulating interest in seamanship'. He would 'authorize the Navy Department to receive the *Svaap* under conditions that may comply with existing law'.

We at once resumed negotiations to have *Svaap* brought back to Panama, but Fate was still against us. Word came at just this time from Tagus Cove. A fishing vessel stopped there and wirelessed that *Svaap* had been pirated and left in very bad condition. The wireless said that she was not worth even towing cost to Panama. This was the final blow. I was unable to realize that *Svaap* had very nearly reached the end of her long voyage. Regretfully we abandoned all hope of bringing her back.

The yacht *Vagabondia* visited Tagus Cove a little later and found that the report had been true. She was in very bad shape and Mr. Mellon had his crew salvage her engine, to save that much for me, and he turned

the hull over to our Norwegian friends of Academy
Bay. I was glad at any rate if they could make some
use of her and care for the hull until we returned to
finish our work down there. I still had hopes of bringing
her home somehow, sometime.

Then the enormously bulky long-distance correspondence about her took a new turn. The Ecuadorean governor of the Galapagos had come over to Academy Bay
and confiscated the *Svaap*, claiming that the Norwegians
to whom I gave her had no right to her. Every mail
day, which is once a month here in Tahiti, brought new
pleas and counter-pleas. The Norwegians wrote. Their
friends wrote for them. Good old Admiral Crosley came
to the front again and did what he could. The legation
in Panama added their share. The Ecuadoreans wrote.
I wrote, sending new papers, legalized by the consul
. . . It seemed for a while that everybody in six countries
were doing nothing but dictating endless correspondence
about poor old *Svaap*. And *Svaap* herself was being
mauled about between Academy Bay and Wreck Bay
where the governor is stationed. The Norwegians
claimed the governor wanted the *Svaap* for his own use.
The government claimed the Norwegians had no legal
right to her. The last mail boat brought word that the
governor had possession of her, that he had let her go
on the beach at Wreck Bay and that she had been dam-
aged still further. In a roundabout way I have heard
that he then had her towed by the old *San Cristobel* to
Guayaquil, where I believe she now lies, possessed by

the Ecuadorean government, or by the Galapagos governor personally, I am not sure which. Admiral Crosley writes: 'I understand they considered it necessary to man the *Svaap* with seven men when she was taken to Guayaquil. It is ironic that the ketch which you sailed around the world with one man should need a crew of seven while under tow for five hundred miles!'

But I doubt if even that is the end. I fully expect to hear by the next mail day — which incidentally will also see the departure of this manuscript — that the *Svaap* has become involved in even more complications. I have already a whole section of a filing cabinet taken up by the reams of correspondence on the subject. At last I have reached the point where I give up. I have loved the *Svaap* more than you would believe it possible to love an inanimate object. I shall always love her. But it has become too much for me. They will have to fight it out among themselves. Possibly some day I may get her back again. Stranger things have happened. And if I do I shall have her made like new again and brought to an honourable resting-place.

Had it not been for the mislaid letter — such a very small thing to have sealed her fate — she would even now have found her final peaceful anchorage. Instead she is an abused hull, haggled over by miscellaneous South American and Scandinavian gentlemen. It is a bitter end — if it is the end — for the brave little *Svaap* who conquered all the oceans and made herself a shining place in the history of small ships. For she was the smallest little vessel that ever circumnavigated the world on her own bottom, under her own sail, in all history.

Ofaipapa, Tahiti
September 25th, 1935